YOUTH
LEADERSHIP

THE UNTAPPED
RESOURCE

REV. DR. PAULA MADDOX

Attention Schools, Educational Centers, and Businesses

Copies of *Youth Leadership: The Untapped Resource* are available at quantity discounts with bulk purchases for educational, business, or sales promotional uses. For information regarding bulk purchases, please forward inquiries to *kingkidscollection@gmail.com*.

Editor: Heather Plym
heatheranne481516@gmail.com
Book Cover Design
www.fiverr.com/burconur
Book format: Sam Okike
www.fiverr.com/psalmyy

ISBN: 978-1-7379669-0-6

KKC

KING KIDS
COLLECTION

DEDICATION

This book is dedicated to my beloved, Adonai, who is the Creator and inspiration of my works. Also, my beloved son who launched his first business in 1990 at eight years of age. I pray this book is a source of encouragement for my grandson, Yosiyah, and all young leaders, who inspire the world in the most profound ways.

ACKNOWLEDGMENTS

This book was given to me through Divine inspiration to acknowledge and express gratitude for the intelligent, multi-talented, inspiring youth and young adults I have met along my journey. The younger generations continue to inspire me to keep growing and maturing into a better version of myself.

A special thank you and acknowledgment to Regent University for their prayers, scholarly guidance, and encouragement. Because of the unconditional support and inspiring faculty at Regent University, I successfully filed and secured my first trademark through the U. S. Patent and Trademark Office. In addition, I want to express my heartfelt thanks and appreciation to my family, friends, cohort, neighbors, ministers, prophets, coaching clients, and publishing team for their support, patience, expertise, and prayers.

TABLE OF CONTENTS

1

YOUTH LEADERSHIP AND COMMUNITY PRACTICE

The most valuable and enduring asset in the world today is our youth. The problems facing our world today are staggering, yet we continue to ignore this essential tool in our arsenal that would allow us to reach sustainable solutions. Our youth are leaders now and tomorrow. They are the most critical resource available for constructive, dynamic, and sustainable solutions and for honest and authentic feedback on an adults' performance. Youth can influence, persuade, speak authentically, and share impactful viewpoints for society and the world. Yet, this powerful resource remains untapped. When will we learn to listen and harvest this valuable resource?

Our children are our greatest treasure and our families' legacies, and they need us to pour into them to grow and thrive into adulthood. They depend upon our love, nutrients, and knowledge. According to Youth Business International, approximately "18,190" young entrepreneurs launched businesses in the United States in 2020.[1] In addition, "13,036" youth were also matched with business mentors the same year.[2] To provide business mentors to our youth is significant and encouraging news, especially since the world was wrapped within the clutches of a global pandemic, resulting in a worldwide lockdown. Our youth moving forward during a pandemic is a testament to their talent, determination, creativity, and ingenious spirit.

The creation of community leadership partnerships is one of several significant ways to develop the youth of today. Multigenerational community partnerships make positive impacts on our youth and communities. Youth learn from mentors and administrators who lead well through example and teach vital skills such as leadership, socialization, emotional intelligence, teamwork, conflict resolution, and decision-making skills. These skills are critical since most of our youth were raised with electronic devices in their hands and interacted through multiple apps and software programs. Millennials, Generation Y, and Z are digital natives, so they developed their social skills through technology; they spend most of their lives in front of screens. Technology is their preferred means of communication, which fails to align with traditional lingo, language, and definitions. Robert Greenleaf, founder of modern servant leadership stated, "Do not assume, because you are intelligent, able, and well-motivated, that you are open to communication, that you know how

---

[1.] "Impact Report 2020," Youth Business International, last modified 2021, https://impact2020.youthbusiness.org/.
[2.] Youth Business International, "Impact Report 2020."

to listen."[3] Communication is a reciprocal process; therefore, it is imperative to listen twice as much as we speak. Maybe that is the purpose of having two ears and one mouth. Intentional socialization is an important foundational skill in perfecting our language, social skills, and emotional intelligence abilities.

Furthermore, youth leadership partnerships are an opportunity for our youth to increase their leadership competencies and community awareness while decreasing isolation, depression, and crime. So, what is leadership, and how do we identify it? There are multiple definitions of leadership. One report prescribes leadership as a process whereby an individual influences a group to achieve a common goal.[4] Ted W. Engstrom describes leadership as "an attitude as well as an action."[5] Engstrom further explains that the quality of leadership:

- provides vision
- deals with concepts
- exercises faith
- seeks for effectiveness
- influences for good among potential resources
- provides direction
- thrives on finding opportunity[6]

In addition, every situation or circumstance is part of our leadership training in the kingdom of God. According to Luke 2:41-52, Jesus began His kingdom leadership in His youth by

---

[3.] Robert Greenleaf, Servant Leadership: A Journey Into the Nature of Legitimate Power and Greatness (NewYork: Paulist Press, 2002).
[4.] P. G Northouse, *Leadership: Theory and practice 6th ed.* (Thousand Oaks: SAGE, 2019).
[5.] Ted W. Engstrom, *The Making of a Christian Leader* (Grand Rapids: Zondervan, 1976).
[6.] Ibid.

teaching in the temple in Jerusalem at the age of 12. The adult teachers and everyone who heard Him "were amazed at His [level of] understanding and knowledge."[7] This example demonstrates the importance of youth leadership. Leadership programs for youth encourage the development of leadership concepts related to community action and social equity.[8] Globally, multiple youth leaders are making an impact through their courageous leadership. Here are just a few accomplishments in recent years:

- **Malala Yousafzai.** A native of Pakistan and one of the youngest recipients of the Nobel Peace Prize for her work in gender equality.[9] She is a survivor of an assassination attempt in 2012 at 15 years of age.

- **Gitanjali Rao.** A young scientist who created multiple inventions with practical uses in the STEM field, particularly technological and medicinal advancement. She specifically invented a device to measure lead amounts in water in Flint, Michigan. She is the first-ever voted Time Magazine Kid of the Year.[10]

- **Greta Thunberg.** The 16-year-old Swedish environmentalist who crossed oceans in a more environmentally friendly boat to lead climate strikes in numerous countries.[11]

---

[7] Luke 2:47 (New International Version).

[8] Andrea Edelman et. al., "Youth development and Youth leadership: A Background Paper," National Collaborative on Workforce and Disability for Youth (June 2004): 4.

[9] "Malala Yousafzai Biographical," Nobel Peace Prize Foundation, last modified 2014, https://www.nobelprize.org/prizes/peace/2014/yousafzai/biographical/

[10] "Meet Time's First Ever Kid of the year," *Time*, December 3, 2020, https://time.com/5916772/kid-of-the-year-2020/.

[11] "Greta Thunberg Foundation Donates to People Fighting the Climate Crisis in Africa," *Solar Sister*, September 23rd, 2020, https://solarsister.org/greta-thunberg-foundation-donates-to-people-fighting-the-climate-crisis-in-africa/.

- **Grace Beverly**. A 24-year-old graduate of Oxford University. She is the CEO of Shreddy, a fitness and recipe app, and Tala, a sustainable activewear brand launched in 2019. Forbes listed her in the Under-30 commerce list. Lastly, she is estimated to have a net worth of $4 million.[12]
- **Cory Nieves**. A 6-year-old who launched "Mr. Cory's Cookies" to help his mother purchase a car and not depend on public transit. The company has a net worth of $1.5 million.[13]

When adults provide children with direction, guidance, discipline, and wisdom, they correctly raise the next generation. When this plan is executed well, the blessings multiply, and society prospers from one generation of impactful leaders to the next. Building and developing our youth is the true meaning of fruitfulness and multiplication, as stated in Genesis 1:22. When one generation of crops fails, the process begins again from ground zero. The land must be prepped with the correct amount of nutrients to sustain a successful crop again. Our youth are leaders and our most excellent harvest of wealth and prosperity. They are the most significant untapped resource that adults allow to lay dormant. It is like having a diamond mine underneath the soil bed of our backyard but taking no action to extract or harvest it. Would we leave it there since it is not bothering anyone? Or would we investigate ways to bring the diamonds to the surface to examine, appraise, and build wealth?

12. "Forbes Profile: Grace Beverley," *Forbes*, last modified 2021, https://www.forbes.com/profile/gracebeverley/?sh=a0fda8bd8a4e
13. "Our Story," Mr. Cory's Cookies, last modified 2021, https://mrcoryscookies.com/pages/our-story.

Our youth are intelligent and ingenious resources. They offer authentic, candid, and transparent questions and feedback to situations. For instance, I remember speaking with a parent who came home from a long day at the office at a technology company. The father followed his routine of greeting his wife, changing into more relaxing attire, and finally entering his son's room to ask how his day at school was. The son shared with his father the events of the day, and at the end of the conversation, the son asked a question of his father. He asked his father for a computer and explained the reasons for needing one. The son evaluated his situation long before he broached the topic with his father, and he explained his reasoning like a well-seasoned attorney speaking about a court case to a presiding judge. The father considered all the information and felt his 8-year-old son could wait until the following year. In the father's mind, there was no immediate need to purchase a computer for his son right now. However, the father offered an option to his son. He told his son that if there was a pressing need for the computer, then he should think of ways to earn money to purchase the computer himself. The son respected his father's decision and remarks; they proceeded downstairs to enjoy dinner as a family.

A month later, the father completed his habitual routine after coming home from work: he greeted his wife and changed into relaxing attire. Before going downstairs for dinner, he opened the door to his son's room to ask about his day and see how he was doing. The father was amazed to see a new computer on his son's desk. He asked his son how did he acquire the computer? The son explained that he took his father's earlier proposal as a challenge and called friends and family members to ask if he could perform errands, odd jobs, or work for them in exchange for monetary compensation. One family member was an entrepreneur and business owner and felt aerial photography from drones would increase her business revenue. However, she had no idea how to operate the drone or use it to its full capacity. The 8-year-old did not either! Regardless, he promised to study the manual and conduct research, so he could operate it and get paid for his services. The young son produced amazing results for the family member, and she compensated him. The pay he earned allowed him to purchase parts to build his computer, and his father was looking at the result on the desk in his room.

The father ignited an entrepreneurial spirit and activated a seed of leadership in his son. The father had financial means to purchase a computer for his son the same day he asked, but he did not. The father wanted to activate something bigger, better, and sustainable in his son. The son benefitted by challenging himself to be entrepreneurial, increase his sales pitch and business acumen, expand his effective communication skills, and increase his knowledge of engineering and technology. Multiple lessons and benefits are extracted from this small act, and they will create a strong foundation to build upon. For example, it is not necessary for parents to feel obliged to purchase every item requested from the youth. Parents should leave room for their children to fully use their creativity, imagination, generate innovative ideas, strategic thinking, and planning skills to initiate entrepreneurial efforts. They should encourage their youth to increase their communication, teaming, partnering, and business skills to attain their goals. This sets them up well for future success because every company employing them will expect the same and will not spoon-feed daily instructions for their job tasks. Our response to our youth lays strong foundations for which tomorrow's CEOs are built.

Adults and parents should encourage youth to lead in all activities in mainstream society and at home. Youth involvement in problem-solving and decision-making processes builds their confidence, strategic planning, and thinking skills. Research reflects multiple benefits in developing youth leadership: increasing self-esteem, preventing risky behavior, and serving as a springboard for maturing youth into successful and responsible adults.[14] Unfortunately, many adolescents are not. given an opportunity or invited to participate as leaders, and there are far too few developmental leadership programs available for adolescents. Youth leaders require a chance to master their skills in a safe environment where they can foster awareness and interaction at home, school, community, and work. Adults are responsible for nurturing and sustaining youth leaders, ensuring that they have ample opportunities to grow, and helping them master their leadership skills in impactful ways.

While the global crisis has altered the paradigm of global leadership, resulting in a considerable shift and awareness of diversity, equity, and inclusion, we need to advocate for the youth. This shift brought the world to a higher level of under-

[14.] J. A. Van Linden and C. I. Fertman, "Youth Leadership: A Guide to Understanding Leadership Development in Adolescents," *Adolescence* 33, no. 131 (Fall 1998): 720.

standing on multiple international platforms. Yet, are we as diverse, equitable, and inclusive as we think? Global leaders need to invite youth leaders' voices to be heard because inclusive leaders possess adaptive mindsets, optimize the talents of everyone, and build trust among the group. Are we giving our youth a reason to trust leaders and adults? How can our youth learn to trust elders when adults block opportunities for youth to develop and be heard as leaders?

Seemingly, adults operate unknowingly in a different type of segregated society, and the uninvited guests are being shunned primarily because of their age. It appears our youth are discriminated against and restricted due to age, which is outside of their control. So, what lessons did adults learn from history, particularly the Civil Rights Era? It appears that there are more lessons to extract from our past errors. The most significant offense is the lesson adults are now teaching our youth, which is age discrimination. How different this perspective will appear when adult leaders age into retirement and youth leaders, who were encouraged to be silent, must now speak for them? It will be an interesting commentary.

Therefore, adults are responsible for ensuring our youth develop a sense of civic responsibility and gain an international understanding of issues facing our world today. Youth need a fertile breeding ground to increase their cultural agility through awareness and respect of foundational principles impacting world politics, religions, and social groups. Through civic and community projects, they will gain critical thinking skills and awareness through diverse perspectives. Through age-appropriate programming, youth can learn to scale their negotiation skills, conflict resolution, effective communication, teaming, and collaborative initiatives.

Naturally, confident youth, at all ages, grow into confident adult leaders. It is comforting to know that leadership is an ageless human characteristic. Often, infants, toddlers, and children show signs of leadership by their ability to focus. For example, children soon find ways to crawl out of cribs, stack toys and blocks to leap out of playpens, open doors, unlock latches, scale barriers, or reach objects intentionally placed out of their reach. Adults often label children's behavior negatively, such as stubbornness, aggressiveness, troublemaking, and mischievousness. However, families and the community could reap considerable benefits if they view these behaviors as skills of focus, analysis, problem-solving, cognitive agility, analytical, strategic, and leadership. What can they do to accelerate these leadership skills in the youth; how can they delegate responsibilities, assign relevant stretch assignments to them, and build their strategic, negotiation, and analytical skills? These are the skills of future Chief Operating Officers (CEOs).[15] These are the skills desired in leaders today and tomorrow. These are also the skills youth can begin to acquire and emulate now.

Leadership training begins at birth, whether we recognize it for what it is or not. However, any new parent can relate to the following scenario. First-time parents experience a paradigm shift after the newborn arrives. The entire household shifts into a new normal once the infant is home. The birth of a child is a natural disruption and establishes new schedules for

---

15. Steven N. Kaplan and Morten Sorensen, "Are CEOs Different?" *The Journal of Finance* 76, no. 4 (2021): 1773.

everyone. The infant leverages power based on the response of the parents, and the parents adjust. When the infant cries, someone will attend to their needs and determine why the child is crying through elimination. Is the infant hungry, sleepy, colicky, hurting, needs changing, or wants to be held? Who has taken the lead in this scenario, and what is taking place? On one level, neural connections link the brain nerve cells; when the nerve cells connect, the brain creates associations between ideas, thoughts, and bits of information, which enables us to process and comprehend our surroundings.[16] From as early as two months of age, infants make mental and physical postural adjustments, demonstrating their ability to anticipate actions through simple observation of others' behavior.[17] Infants utilize the same available resource adults have at their disposal: the brain. Just think about what our youth can accomplish with such a mindset as they mature into responsible adults.

In addition, youth leadership is vital to every segment of society, including their peers. Notable news journalists and mothers note female youth ages eight through fourteen, which is an adolescent period, experience a thirty percent drop in confidence.[18] Since youth listen to their peers and often tune out adults, why not increase youth leadership and provide them an opportunity to build up their peers' confidence and skills? Youth leadership should be a mainstream expectation in every family,

---

[16.] Amy K. Hutchens, Brain Brilliant: Increase Your Personal and Professional Profit (Atlanta: Amy K. Publishing, 2002): 18.

[17.] Claire Monroy, Chen Chi-Hsin, Derek Houston, .and Chen Yu. "Action Prediction during real-time parent-infant Interactions." *Developmental Science* (2021): 2.

[18.] Kelly Wallace, "A 'Confidence Code' for Girls: 5 Ways to Build up Our Daughters," *CNN*, May 21st, 2018, https://www.cnn.com/2018/05/21/health/girls-confidence-code-parenting/index.html.

community, and social and civic arena because it offers diversity to existing multi-generational teams. Youth can share alternative perspectives, viewpoints, and observations to stretch, refine, and increase adult awareness. They bring value to conversations and speak from a courageous place of authenticity and transparency, which adults sometimes lose due to fear and high risk. Young adults offer perspectives for the greater good of society, unlike adults who may fail to exercise this option due to fear or threat. Suppose youth can resolve such minor problems with strategic thinking, planning skills, agility, resilience, analytical thinking, focus, attention, and concentration. In that case, there is no limit to their contributions to solving social challenges and problems.

Young adults possess a keen level of awareness, which often benefits our communities and society. In 2010, a survey conducted by Junior Achievement reflected that "two in three teens (65%) are confident they will land their dream job one day; however, 84% said they would forego the perfect job for the opportunity to make a difference in the world."[19] That is a powerful revelation. Youth are inclined to express and demonstrate acts of compassion and empathy toward others, resulting in higher levels of social intelligence. Anwer et. al. defines social intelligence as the person's ability to be intelligent in his and others' relationship and the capacity of persons being socially aware, empathetic, and having the social skills related to self-preservation and concern.[20]

---

[19] "Teens Confident They Will Land Dream Jobs," *Youth Market Alerts* 22, no. 6 (2010): 8.
[20] Moazama Anwer, et al., "The Moderating Role of Social Intelligence in Explaining Attachment Style and Emotional Intelligence Among Young Adults," *Pakistan Journal of Psychology* 48, no. 2 (2017): 12.

In addition, Riggio and Reichard examined broad interpersonal skills such as empathy, social skills, and emotional intelligence to predict the effectiveness and emergence of leadership within individuals.[21] For instance, most children are empathetic and express compassion for others. They often hurt when they see others in pain, and many life lessons become evident when watching children and youth interact in classrooms and team sports. They often resolve complex issues and challenges among themselves through influence, persuasion, and negotiation. They find ways to be inclusive, share classroom resources, and come to the aid of a peer. That is youth leadership at work.

Furthermore, all adults began as babies and youth who possessed volumes of confidence and resiliency. It is exciting and amusing to watch toddlers and children accomplish monumental feats when they are focused on getting their hands on their favorite food or toys. They are creative and inventive when they want something, such as stacking objects and scaling barriers to overcome challenges. They accomplish near Olympic-scale feats when they focus on their target and pursue their mission without regard or thought of risk or consequence. The same resiliency, creativeness, and inventiveness follows them through their adolescence and teenage years. The Lemelson-MIT Invention Index conducted research in 2008 and reflected that "American teens are confident enough to invent solutions to the world's

---

[21.] Ronald E. Riggio and Rebecca J. Reichard, "The Emotional and Social Intelligences of Effective Leadership: An Emotional and Social Skill Approach," *Journal of Managerial Psychology* 23, no. 2 (2008): 169-185.

most significant challenges, such as protecting our natural resources and environment."[22] Young adults can add substantial
value toward resolving many problems and challenges facing
the world today because their intelligence stems from a more
straightforward place, uncomplicated with layers of fear and
risk. They need more opportunities to build this muscle at home,
at school, and in community organizations. They are indeed an
untapped resource we must learn to value, mine, refine, and
polish like diamonds.

Our youth play an essential role in society, and adults are
responsible for ensuring our youth are growing and thriving in
fertile gardens of nutrient-enriched soil. By tilling their gardens
with knowledge, responsibility, accountability, and engagement,
adults help build their self-esteem, which is closely associated
with their well-being[23].

Youth are not only tech-savvy, brutally honest, and observant;
they offer multiple levels of value to any situation. For instance,
various cultures know and embrace their youthful resource by
requiring them to interrupt their academic journey to serve in
the military for a period before resuming their schooling. Multiple
youth leaders in history made significant impacts and improved
the world. Here are just a few examples of the value young adults
bring when they are tapped and valued as a resource:

- Edward Goodrich Acheson received his first patent at
  the age of 17 by the United States (U. S.) Patent Office for

---

[22] "US Teens Confident in their Inventiveness; Hands-on, Project-Based Learning
Needed," Lemelson-MIT Program, January 17th, 2008, sciencedaily.com.

[23] Fatima Hashmi, Aftab Hira, José Moleiro Martins, Mário Nuno Mata, Hamza Ahmad
Qureshi, António Abreu, and Pedro Neves Mata, "The Role of Self-Esteem, Optimism,
Deliberative Thinking and Self-Control in Shaping the Financial Behavior and Financial
Well-being of Young Adults," *PloS One* 16, no. 9 (2021): 18.

"Improvements in the Process of Mining Coal, Ore, Clay, etc."[24] He was forced to leave boarding school and work to support his family. He achieved this monumental feat because "his father impressed upon him the value of studying mechanics and accomplishing something of value."[25]

- In 1836, Samuel Colt was 22 years of age when he obtained a U. S. Patent for the Colt revolver.[26]

- King Josiah, a grandson of Manasseh, King of Judah, ascended to the throne at eight years of age and reigned in Jerusalem for 31 years.[27]

- Alexander the Great was a cavalry commander at 16 years of age and king by twenty.[28] He built new cities in the lands he conquered including Alexandria in Egypt. He created one of the largest empires of the ancient world, stretching from Greece to northwestern India.

- Jason Li is the 15-year-old Founder of iReTron, an electronics company encouraging cell phone owners to surrender their electronic devices for cash. The older devices are sold abroad instead of contaminating landfills.[29]

[24.] Edwin Wildman, Famous Leaders of Industry: The Life Stories of Boys who have Succeeded (Boston: Page Company, 1921): 5.
[25.] Wildman, Famous Leaders of Industry, 5.
[26.] Wildman, 52.
[27.] 2 Chronicles 34:1 (New King James Version).
[28.] Justin D. Lyons, Alexander the Great and Hernán Cortés: Ambiguous Legacies of Leadership (Blue Ridge Summit: Lexington Books, 2015): 23.
[29.] "Teen Entrepreneur Wins Big: 15-Year-Old Founder of Online E-Reuse Business Named Next Teen Tycoon by VerticalResponse: Three Winning Teens Receive Prizes Worth $10,000 to Grow their Businesses," PR Newswire, March 22nd, 2012, https://www.prnewswire.com/news-releases/teen-entrepreneur-wins-big-15-year-old-founder-of-online-e-reuse-business-named-next-teen-tycoon-by-verticalresponse-143801496.html.

- Catherine Cook created "MyYearbook.com" in 2005 and became a millionaire at 17 years old.[30]

There are also multiple untold success stories achieved by youth from centuries ago to our modern day. Since there is no limit to the human mind, the world cannot afford to ignore the untapped resource of children and youth.[31] Our minds are a complex machine of tissue, neural pathways, messaging nerve cells, and neural circuitry. Our brains are a complex universe designed to be used to its most remarkable capacity through wisdom and sound decision-making.[32] Our brains continuously grow, adapt, change, and re-wire in repetitive patterns to function at their best and keep us alive.[33] The brain typically registers over thirty-six thousand images per hour and our eyes can archive thirty million bits of information per second, which means the world needs this resource.[34] Therefore, leaders can explore multiple ways to learn and expand their knowledge through a culture of innovation, creativity, adaptability, and sustainable growth.[35] Leadership is a mindset and not a destination. Our youth are full of wonder, ideas, and active imaginations. They are disbelievers of restriction and limitation. They are willing to test their limits with courage, not fear, and they are risk averse.

Since the youth carry a spirit of courage and fearlessness, they are ideal for focus groups and as early adopters of technology and other products. Some companies already recognize

---

[30] Catherine Cook and Sandy Fertman Ryan, "I Became a Millionaire at 17!" *Girls' Life* 15, no. 6 (2009): 82.

[31] Cook and Ryan, 82.

[32] Hutchens, *Brain Brilliant*, 18-19.

[33] Hutchens, *Brain Brilliant*, 18-19.

[34] Ibid.

[35] Chambers Brothers, *Language and Pursuit of Leadership Excellence* (Naples, F.L.: New Possibilities Press, 2015).

the value of youth and place them in controlled conditions to observe their actions and interactions with prototypes of new products or services. The young testers surely give the product designers honest, transparent responses to questions and an earful regarding their expectations and imaginations. All the information gathered from the control group is invaluable. The data is analyzed in multiple ways and discussed to create the next blueprint, design, and prototype.

However, product and tech companies hire numerous psychologists and mental health experts to market both beneficial and harmful products to the youth. Companies study lifestyle, habits, and brain activity to understand patterns, inquiry, peer pressure, feelings, and taste of selling toys, animated objects, drugs, liquor, and e-cigarettes. Is it best to develop youth leaders for the benefit of society, or watch them sink into exploitation and addiction? Instead of exploiting or discriminating against youth leaders, adults need to raise up the next generation of leaders with excellent team-building skills, innovative thinking and decision-making capabilities, emotional intelligence, conflict resolution, negotiating and bargaining skills, and a strong perspective.

2

STRONG TEAM-BUILDING SKILLS

In order to gain excellent team-building skills, all leaders must possess a hefty dose of self-awareness. They should be committed to improving their performance, assessing their progress, and using discernment to determine what is or is not working well. It is crucial for leaders to self-reflect and raise their self-awareness. Leaders and followers are co-dependent on each other; however, they fulfill separate roles. Their relationship is one of teamwork, collaboration, and continuous growth as they focus on impact and improvement in common areas of interest.

Leaders are only as strong as the teams supporting their network. For instance, international sport team coaches and Olympic coaches are only as successful as the team they coach. In a business setting, this holds true as well; CEOs and leaders are often asked to share nuggets of wisdom through public forums, town hall meetings, and interviews by reporters. Unfortunately, some leaders consciously take full credit for the entire business and corporation when credit should be assigned to the teams and networks that execute actions to yield results. Still, wise and discerning leaders give more credit to their workforce and team by acknowledging their investment and hard work. The wise and discerning leader admits to hiring experts and high-potential workers who perform their roles well while the leader asks the right questions that lead to the best decisions.

Moreover, effective leadership is evidenced by followership. Followership is formed when individuals accept the influence of others while striving toward a common goal.[36] Therefore, followership is as crucial as leadership. The followership executes the goals and agenda of the leader. Leaders rarely accomplish numerous achievements alone, working in a vacuum without any support from others. A closer examination of followership requires self-reflection and reveals why they follow specific leaders.

Followership is as critical as leadership; one cannot exist without the other, and it is a relationship of co-dependency. Ira Chaff states, one component of *courageous followership* is "the degree of support a follower gives a leader and the degree to which the follower is willing to challenge the leader's behavior or policies if these are endangering the organization's purpose or undermining its values."[37] In addition, courageous followers benefit from the leader who serves as their mentor. Yet, the follower should also be open and willing to teach the leader through constructive feedback.[38] Exemplary followers add value

---

36. Northouse, Leadership: Theory and practice.
37. Ira Chaleff, The Courageous Follower: Standing Up to & for our Leaders 2 ed. (San Francisco: Berrett-Koehler, 2003).
38. Ibid.

to teams and organizations by executing critical thinking skills and excelling above and beyond the expectation of leaders and organizations.[39]

Some followers prescribe it is easier to follow than to lead, but research disapproves this theory. Followership is not a "safe alternative to leadership identity" because followership is encapsulated with risks.[40] People collectively construct identities, which determine the paradigm of the leader-follower relationship and their interactions.[41] Followership requires constant observation and evaluation of the leaders' intent because followers directly relate to their public perception. Therefore, followers must track and sync with the leader to determine if they still fully align with the leader's values, morals, ethics, and intent. They must notice when shifts occur. If followers are not attentive to the leaders who they hold a close association with through investment and reputation, the brand of the follower may be tarnished or questioned. Followers should always have the courage to make inquiries and ask questions of those they follow. If leaders shun inquiries and questions for clarification and learning, followers should objectively focus on the intent of the leader with discernment.

In contrast, Jesus exemplifies an excellent leader who continually encouraged His followers to work together and to demonstrate compassion, mercy, forgiveness, and encouragement. Jesus had a strong team of followers even though they

---

[39.] R.E. Kelley, *The Power of Followership: How to Create Leaders People Want to Follow* (New York, N.Y.: Doubleday, 1992).

[40.] Ibid.

[41.] Magnus Larsson and Mie Femø Nielsen, "The Risky Path to a Followership Identity: From Abstract Concept to Situated Reality," *International Journal of Business Communication* 58, no. 1 (2017): 9.

worked in less-than-ideal conditions, walking from region to region. His followers included men and women, who camped near water and natural resources in tents while witnessing to others and learning from our Savior. If we think working with a small diverse team is challenging, can you imagine how challenging it was for 12 men from opposing vocations to work through daily challenges in the wilderness? Despite their differences, they camped together, prepared, and ate meals together, shared resources to survive, and labored together for over a year. Oftentimes, we find it overwhelming to deal with others unlike ourselves for a two-hour meeting or an eight-hour workday!

Followers require specific skills, discernment, commitments, and responsibilities to themselves and the leaders they follow. Courageous and responsible followers must:

- deploy multiple skills to exercise faith in self and keenly observe everything for analysis and discernment.
- exercise their ability to speak power to the truth and eliminate blind spots, which enables them to see clearly and objectively.
- set standards to model values, morals, and behaviors of strong, influential leaders.
- use their power to react to situations morally and professionally regardless of the threat.
- use their skills to communicate effectively and organize others with like minds or common causes.

- execute their power to withdraw their support of leaders violating their values, morals, beliefs, and ethics.[42]

However, hidden within every follower is a leader.[43] It is the mindset and thinking processes that separate a leader from a follower. The leader possesses a unique mental attitude that creates a strong sense of self-worth, faith, confidence, strength, and belief in possibilities.[44] Dr. Myles Munroe posited, "the spirit of leadership is birthed in the womb of a personal revelation within the leader and manifests itself in specific and characteristic qualities."[45] Every human has leadership capacity, but most will not activate the seed within them and cultivate it. Leadership is a product of divine inspiration and aligns with purpose. Dr. Munroe posited "our beliefs are a product of our thoughts; thoughts create our beliefs; beliefs create our convictions; convictions create our attitude, attitude controls our perception, and perception dictates our behavior."[46] Leadership is a trusted position given by the follower, and it is an attitude of the heart.[47] The difference between a leader and a follower is the individual's mindset, heart, courage, and philosophy.

Furthermore, the most effective leaders know the magnitude of results gained when leadership successfully incorporates teamwork. Teamwork is an essential skill needed throughout our life's journey, including academia, military deployment,

---

42. Chaleff, The Courageous Follower, 18-19.
43. Myles Munroe, The Spirit of Leadership: Cultivating the Attributes that Influence Human Action (New Kensington, P.A. Whitaker House, 2018).
44. Munroe, Spirit of Leadership.
45. Munroe, Spirit of Leadership.
46. Munroe, Spirit of Leadership.
47. Ibid.

employment, and our entrepreneurial ventures. Teamwork comprises two or more individuals working towards a common goal with set roles and role interdependencies.[48] Teamwork requires a collaboration of individuals who gather for a common goal. It can "significantly improve performance, effectiveness, efficiency, morale, job satisfaction, unity of purpose, communications, innovative thinking, quality, speed, and loyalty" to a cause.[49] Teamwork is the skill needed in pandemics and other challenging times of dynamic change. Leaders and businesses need more than just the gathering of individuals; each person needs to possess the spirit of teamwork and collaboration for a more significant objective. For example, the military is the most significant demonstration of the strength, fortitude, and trust gained through teamwork and leadership initiatives.

Yet, teaming is an important attribute for any group of individuals. It is important enough for parents to teach it to children early in life. Parents often encourage infants and toddlers to share food and toys with others, so the principles of sharing and teaming are instilled early. It is essential to introduce such moral characteristics as soon as possible.

There are multiple benefits of learning how to team, partner, and collaborate well. Recent studies reveal more about the development of interpersonal relationships. A team-member exchange (TMX) impacts the effectiveness of the emotional

[48] J.E. Mathieu et. al., "A Century of Work Teams," *Journal of Applied Psychology* 102, no. 3 (2017): 458.
[49] D.D. Warrick, "What Leaders can Learn about Teamwork and Developing High Performance Teams from Organization Development Practitioners," *Performance Improvement* 55, no. 3 (2016): 13.

intelligence (EQ) of the team.[50] EQ is the ability to "process emotional information," which contributes to top performance and the ability to "influence interpersonal interactions" with individuals and teams.[51] Processing emotional information is imperative to gauge and discern others when executing job tasks, negotiating, strategizing, and partnering with others. Teaming provides an opportunity to increase collaborative relationships, mutual trust, respect, and open communications, which are key skills in business, corporate, and entrepreneurial initiatives. Usually, teaming and collaboration skills are:

- voluntary
- seeking parity among participants
- focusing on mutual goals
- depending on shared responsibility for participation and decision-making
- sharing tools and resources
- sharing accountability for successful outcomes[52]

Teaming skills and the desire to collaborate are particularly important today in the post-COVID era. The world operates in global economies with streamlined and flatter organizations. For example, many companies in the technology industry implemented a flat organizational structure. Workers are expected to team cross-functionally and cross-culturally without a supervisor or manager to resolve team conflicts, disagreements, or

---

[50.] Di Zhao and Wenjun Cai, "When does Emotional Intelligence (EI) Benefit Team-Member Exchange? the Cross-Level Moderating Role of EI-Based Leader-Member Exchange Differentiation," *Career Development International* 26, no. 3 (2021): 391.

[51.] Zhao and Cai, 391.

[52.] Ann E. Knackendoffel. "Collaborative Teaming in the Secondary School," *Focus on Exceptional Children* 40, no 4 (2007): 1.

difficult discussions. Most times, each team is given an objective to resolve, a budget, and a deadline to report results. Several team members are located geographically in other parts of the world; therefore, the team must collaborate and discuss how to manage project objectives and meet regularly despite time zone differences. They must also resolve disagreements and differences of opinion in how to move forward with project goals and job tasks at the same level. The same applies to any personality, ethnic, or cultural differences or biases. Teaming, partnering, and collaborating with internal and external stakeholders is important for career success in any industry. It is especially important in the technology industry where job performance evaluations are scheduled every 30-90 days, and there are no guarantees in high-impact industries. In situations such as this, skills in partnering, negotiation, collaboration, and teaming are paramount and crucial to career success.

Shared leadership concepts are important for leaders to implement and drive results. No one is self-sufficient. Each of us relies on others for something, which is a standard way of life. Humans were created to be interdependent, not independent. Independently, we accomplish little or nothing at all. John Donne once stated, "no man is an island"[53] because we are all connected. Shared leadership shifts our thinking and mindset about teams and organizations as an effective driver of strong performance. Many foundational cultural and social practices are similar and often spring from the same origination point. Therefore, our commonalities provide opportunities to resolve challenges and increase positive impacts throughout the world.

53. John Donne, "No Man is an Island" [Title Derived], Wakefield Express, 2021.

For instance, Jesus had a shared ministry, which included the 12 disciples and many others. Each time Jesus traveled through regions and invited others by stating, "follow me," Jesus shared His leadership and built leadership skills in His followers. Jesus is an incubator or boot camp for others to foster and build leadership skills filled with grace, integrity, ethics, compassion, mercy, forgiveness, and encouragement. If Jesus did not have a shared ministry encouraging and inspiring His followers to emulate his demonstrations and document events they witnessed, where would we be today?

Building strong teams require mutual respect, trust, and sharing of common goals. The strongest teams hold all members accountable for their actions and performance. Leadership accountability is vital and should be demonstrated well regardless of whether others are looking. Every effective team needs accountable leaders to promote cohesiveness and transform society in an impactful way. Accountability enables strong teams to leverage high performance, identify key drivers, and give them a competitive edge.[54] Everyone benefits when teams hold one another accountable.

Fortunately, youth possess the expertise to collaborate, partner, and team better than adults. Youth are honest, transparent, and courageous to participate in discussions. They want their voices and opinions heard, and they desire to create an impact. Youth are imaginative, take risks, increase discovery, and are less inclined to place limits around their abilities. They consider more possibilities, feel it is important to hear every voice,

---

[54] Vince Molinaro, Accountable Leaders: Inspire a Culture Where Everyone Steps Up, Takes Ownership, and Deliver Results (Gildan Media, 2020).

:: 27 ::

and listen to alternative viewpoints. Somewhere along the journey of life, adults stop giving themselves permission to stretch and grow. This lack of progress leads to hindrances, blind spots, inability to execute actionable items and create greater impacts.

3
INNOVATIVE THINKING AND DECISION MAKING

Youth leaders must grow their innovative thinking and decision-making abilities because these vital skills drive progress. Innovative thinking includes flipping your assumptions through: accessing risks, strategic foresight, defining/clarifying objectives, and managing ambiguity. Decision-making includes emotional self-control (emotional intelligence and emotional regulation). These skills and leadership characteristics impact every industry and require us to flip our assumptions. For example, innovative thinking developed the music industry, which began with recorded sound on a phonograph and led to digital downloads today. In the automobile industry, it began with the first steam or gas-powered car in the late 1800s up to the electric vehicle today. Innovative thinkers and leaders will continue to lead every industry to keep businesses thriving.

Our young people are highly intelligent and superb strategic thinkers, and adults should take every available opportunity to support them. My own life proves this. I purchased my first home in 1985, and the developer built it after I signed the contract. As a single mother in the early stages of my career, my finances were stretched thin. I was thankful to God to receive the blessing of a newly built home, but the closing costs wiped out most of my savings. I knew the sacrifice was worth the cost of having my son with me again; my parents cared for him for a few years while I worked two jobs to invest in a home for us. The feeling of living in an unattached home of my own for the first time is indescribable. I did not miss the stomping, bumping, voices, or noises often heard above, below, or beside my apartment unit. My son and I enjoyed new furnishings, including a newly installed carpet. That is where we ate, slept, watched television, played board games, and folded the laundry. I had to save more money to purchase furniture.

In the interim, I noticed my son's interest in a new emerging industry called technology. Computers were becoming available to consumers in the early 1980s, and I was interested in seeing what my son could do with such a machine. I decided to delay the purchase of household furniture and opted to splurge on our first-ever family computer called a Compaq Computer and an ink jet printer. My son took to this new technology like a butterfly to nectar. He began to learn computer code and manipulate software. We began to have more discussions about technology, computers, and software.

My nine-year-old-son wanted to stretch his business and computer skills by launching his first entrepreneurial effort. In the late 1980s, he made 10-12 sample personalized greeting cards, and we placed them in a portfolio. He took his portfolio to school with him each day and returned home each week with orders to fill for payment. This was the beginning of his entrepreneurial journey into the world of business. Incidentally, he has accelerated his learning and inventory of specialized skills since the 1980s, and he has launched multiple successful business ventures and published multiple publications. His infant son is following the same entrepreneurial pathway and has a social webpage and channel on the Internet. Business skills start early and can be introduced in our youth.

It is not surprising our children are often tapped by top corporate conglomerates, cyber-security firms, and the government to test the security of their highly sophisticated software, gaming systems, toy safety, and cyber-security initiatives. Candid and authentic feedback from youth focus groups yield valuable information to produce goods and services by major corporations. Adults should never think youth cannot successfully manage the simplest of tasks at home or in the community.

Recently, I taught classes at the Viking Cooking School featuring local and international menus, and one of the best treats was to teach a weeklong annual kid's camp at the cooking school. It is a rewarding experience for the class attendees and the instructors as we work through demonstrations and recipes together before enjoy a meal together. Some of the kids return each year to learn new international cuisines, and some were new. I was amazed how children could cook so well and understand culinary terms when they could barely reach the granite counters and stove tops of the ranges. Amazingly, some of them cook all the meals at home each week. The children create a menu of weekly meals and prepare a shopping list to give to their parents to purchase all the ingredients. The family enjoys elevated restaurant quality meals at home from their child. Many of the children aspire to attain a culinary career and own restaurants, and I have no doubt they will reach their goals. In many cases, the international dishes that the children prepared in class were superior to the ones prepared by adults. The young chefs taught me a thing or two as well.

Young leaders possess vision and have dreams and plans for life. Their goal plan is like my plan for scuba diving.

- Young leaders select a destination, and they develop plans to hit their target goal. We cannot launch a goal without a destination. Before I scuba dive, I must select a dive site based on my experience level. I must plan for smooth calm waters as well as turbulent, choppy waves or surges. The destination is important because we must ensure we have the equipment, stamina, and tools to reach the destination. Young leaders must take an inventory of their toolbox and acquire additional skills through research, study, or mentors to hit their target. Likewise, I must ensure I have the appropriate dive gear suitable for the water depth of my dive.

- Young leaders should remain in communication with mentors and God. They need to ensure they are aligning with their purpose and God's divine plan for their life. If they do not, they may change course, potentially derail, miss their target, or fall short of their destination. The distractions of the world and other people are always a temptation to take them off course. Likewise, I must remain in communication with my dive buddy and God. Water conditions rapidly change in multi-depth dives and drop offs suddenly appear. It is best to retain eye contact with your dive buddy for safety reasons and monitor air consumption and nitrogen loading. I remain in communication with God to determine the appropriate place and time to dive. When diving in the depths of the ocean, it is best for God to approve of your dive plan.

Moreover, our youth desire an opportunity to engage and participate in meaningful ways and to think innovatively and scale their decision-making skills. Adults can support youth by ensuring they are:

- defining clear objectives
- applying emotional intelligence
- creating a framework to access risk and manage ambiguity
- deploying strategic foresight skills
- developing a mastery of negotiation and bargaining skills

Adults especially need to support and develop youth leaders during this time. The onset of COVID-19 and a global pandemic awakened the world out of its slumber and era of fun to a new reality of purpose and meaning. Many people used the global lockdown for deep thought and self-reflection about the true meaning of their life, the loved ones they lost, and those who remain with them. What is the purpose of it all? Some questioned why they are still here, and if they truly used all the available resources to make their life fruitful or to improve the lives of others in their community?

Some realized they were too self-consumed with their own personal and corporate goals and dreams. They could have invested more in others, especially the youth in their communities. Educational researchers cite the need for a paradigm shift for adult and youth leadership in the global market. Globalization is one of the most important economic, cultural, and social trends of the past century, but the educational curricula does not best support the development of global leadership in our youth.[55] In contrast, youth leadership and mentors shift our youth from victims to victors. The world may reap substantial benefits by encouraging scholarship-centered critical youth studies, especially urban youth, on the injustices plaguing the world.[56]

One substantial benefit is that young leaders bring fresh ideas and perspectives to conversations when they are invited to participate creatively and encouraged to think innovatively about local and global challenges. Youth are quite intuitive even during the global pandemic. For example, Kimberly-Viola Heita is 21 years old and thought 2020 would present opportunities for her to become a student radio presenter at the University of Namibia.[57] However, the pandemic closed her school, but she did not disconnect. Instead, Heita and nearly 100 students used WhatsApp for debate, motivation, and support.[58] Heita posited that 2020 forced her to innovate, collaborate, and

[55.] Ayana Allen-Handy, Shawnna L. Thomas-El, and Kenzo K. Sung, "Urban Youth Scholars: Cultivating Critical Global Leadership Development through Youth-Led Justice-Oriented Research," *The Urban Review* 53 (2020): 270.

[56.] Ibid.

[57.] Nellie Peyton, "Generation COVID: How the Young are Working Round Pandemic-hit Job Market," *Reuters*, January 11, 2021, https://www.reuters.com/article/health-coronavirus-youth-employment/generation-covid-how-the-young-are-working-round-pandemic-hit-job-market.

[58.] Peyton, "Generation COVID."

discover resilience she did not know they had.[59] Likewise, many adults desired to launch businesses before COVID, but could not find clients. After, they found a rich field of digital clients and multiple opportunities to mentor and teach new skills to youth.

Many businesses thrived on traditional business cycles and practices during the pre-COVID era, but things changed. Businesses must focus on innovation and creative thinking to survive in the coming years. The global pandemic forced the world to rely heavily on digital communications to survive and to connect services. The lockdown period taught us how to implement new ways to conduct business, sell products and services, and use existing resources differently to remain ahead of global competition. Which businesses will be early adopters of new innovative ideas? Which ones will be the first out of the gate? Which businesses will be too slow and left in the dust to close their doors permanently? The answers to these questions will involve strategic foresight.

What is strategic foresight? It is a skill each leader must develop to create a roadway into the future. Strategic foresight focuses on the importance of determining alternative futures and creating scenarios to support agile strategies.[60] Strategic foresight provides an opportunity to exercise a choice to create a preferred future based on what is to come.[61] For instance, the

[59.] Peyton, "Generation COVID."
[60.] John Ratcliffe, "Property futures—the Art and Science of Strategic Foresight," *Journal of Property Investment & Finance* 38 (5 (2020): 483.
[61.] James Canton, Future Smart: Managing the Game-Changing Trends That Will Transform Your World (Philadelphia: Da Capo Press, 2016).

U. S. military regularly deploys this skill on and off the battlefields in alignment with their strategic plans and purposes.

Strategic foresight aids young leaders with short and long-term planning initiatives, particularly when it is aligned with strategy.[62] The skill of strategic foresight is regularly implemented in youth leadership initiatives, leadership development programs, and businesses. It allows leaders to observe with intent the signs, signals, and trends of today to gauge and predict future possibilities. Investing time in strategic foresight initiatives gives leaders an advantage over global competitors through outreach beyond the typical one-to-five-year strategic business planning processes.

Strategic foresight is a skill each prospective student and new hire should consider before accepting a position or deciding upon a field of study. Each year, several occupations are no longer needed and fall within a black hole, never to be seen again. For example, society once needed grocery bagging personnel, gas station attendants, scissors grinders, ice cutters, typists, water carriers, elevator operators, film projectionists, milk, and diaper delivery men. Futurists predict occupations that will require modification or elimination in the next ten years because of the advancement of technology and machine learning, including: [63]

- Insurance underwriters
- Photography lab processors
- Receptionists

[62] Simon R. Reese, "Implement Strategic Foresight with Elements of the US army's Operational Art Model." *Strategic Direction* 36, no. 5 (2020): 5.
[63] Kerri Anne Renzulli, "Here are the 15 Job Disappearing the Fastest in the U.S.," *CNBC*, April 28, 2019, https://www.cnbc.com/2019/04/26/the-15-us-jobs-disappearing-the-fastest.html.

- Telemarketers
- Cashiers and bank tellers
- Postmasters and mail superintendents
- Metal pourers and casters
- Motor vehicle electronic equipment installers and repairers
- Watch repairers
- Parking enforcement workers
- Respiratory therapy technicians

All young professionals and students should invest time in strategic foresight or other key performance indicators (KPIs) of time and money into advanced degrees and careers to ensure a return on investment. One of my doctoral professors and other futurists suggest leaders use internet search engines to conduct research upfront. They instruct them to place a topic or subject of interest in the search engine with the year 2030 behind it. Then, leaders should take the time to review the consulting reports populating after the search to find common trends and data regarding the future demand or need. It is advisable to also conduct a second search with the same topic of interest with the year 2050 placed behind it. Then, they review the results to uncover trends and future demand. The same process can be used to determine the lifecycle of a potential business idea or launch of an initiative. These types of searches give leaders information relative to the future possibilities, and the search will produce valuable information regarding other global initiatives being deployed. Global internet searches allow users to investigate global initiatives, leading to ways to regain a market share or the ability to stay ahead of the competition. Strategic foresight is a tool that enables us to increase management and leadership skills personally and professionally. It is an opportunity that leaders cannot afford to dismiss or disregard.

Integrating strategic foresight methods into our scenario planning initiatives increases our ability to stay ahead of the pack. A recent journal article states, *"strategic foresight offers leaders the ability to simultaneously. Monitor external trends and analyze critical internal performance indicators while focusing the organization on a shared vision of the future."*[64] Strategic foresight helps leaders create a shared vision beyond near-term uncertainties that align with strategic actions. Successful leaders make effective decisions by having strategic foresight skills, a destination or target, and a sound plan. They also identify potential derailers. When leaders move with purpose and intention, most familiar places, spaces, and faces must change. It is unlikely others will desire to accelerate their pace to track or sync with someone moving at a rapid pace and pivot in a different direction. If leaders slow down to accommodate the comfortability of others, their plans will be delayed or miss their target.

For example, when an airline files a flight plan, it has a destination to reach before it leaves its point of origin. The pilot has a certain timeframe to leave the tarmac and to arrive at the intended destination to avoid collisions with other flights. The airline cannot afford to constantly delay flight departures, due to late passenger arrivals. Likewise, leaders must remain on

---

[64.] Reese, "Implement Strategic Foresight," 5.

course with their plans and not allow others to cause unnecessary delays.

Successful leaders do not have to 'check-in 'with others who want to inquire about their plans for the sake of being nosey. Leaders encourage others to pursue their plans and empower them to create a plan and target to hit. They must frequently evaluate the landscape to identify possible derailers, so their attention is not diverted. Leaders do not have much time to be entertained or act as a source of entertainment for others. Instead, they must remain focused and determined to make an impact and improve conditions for others. Someone's life will be improved by their success.

An example of this is when I remained mindful of timing while in graduate school. When in school or focused on any goal, timing is defined and used differently. It appears to be fleeting, and students are mindful to continuously schedule around, meet, and beat deadlines. We must vigorously protect our time and diligently guard our boundaries. I found a technique used by one of my professors as an irritating nuisance when I was in class. However, God urged me to take another look at the technique because it accomplishes a larger goal. My professor used a cooking timer for class discussions to ensure every student had an opportunity to speak and share insights on a topic. It was a useful and effective instructional aid in class, so I deployed the same technique for personal phone calls. I kept a cooking timer near me when working or studying, and I politely told personal callers they had 3 minutes to speak to me with a 30-second wrap up before the kitchen timer buzzes. At that time, I would end the phone call. This may sound harsh, but it accomplishes several essential goals.

- I recovered valuable time to execute my divine purpose.
- I ensured others respected my time with a focused inquiry and not idle chit-chat and gossip.
- I encouraged others to reclaim their time and make it count.
- If I do not respect my time, no one else will.
- It reminded me to value time and make an impact as I remained focused on my divine purpose.

Leaders must respect their time and stand by their decisions. They need to eencourage their followership and others to ask questions and make valid inquiries. Questions are not an issue when followers move with intention and purpose, which allows leaders to explain their intentions without the need to defend. Others can only make assumptions unless they address their inquiry to the leader or someone who is designated to speak on the leader's behalf.

4

EMOTIONAL INTELLIGENCE

The mental and physical well-being of youth leaders is vital to the leadership of individuals and their followership. Emotional intelligence (EQ) impacts the health and well-being of leaders because it is the ability to understand and manage emotions and influence the emotions of others. Leaders with high levels of EQ often are high performers. Career Builder.com surveyed employers and 71% of them valued EQ over intelligence quotient (IQ).[65] Leaders with high EQ possess skills to become great entrepreneurs because they likely remain calm under pressure, resolve conflict effectively, and respond to others with empathy.[66] EQ equips entrepreneurs with skills to make wise decisions in the face of emotionally difficult situations, maintain motivation and persistence, and effectively build

---

[65.] Jared S. Allen et. al., "What Matters More for Entrepreneurship Success? A meta-analysis Comparing General Mental Ability and Emotional Intelligence in Entrepreneurial Settings," *Strategic Entrepreneurship Journal* 15, no. 3 (2021): 352-376.

[66.] Allen et. al., "Entrepreneurship Success?" 352-376.

and manage relationships and networks.[67] Successful entrepreneurs should deploy the necessary skills to sustain successful business ventures and make wise business investments.

Industry experts recommend nine actions youth can implement and do to increase their EQ. It is vitally important for youth to find successful and productive ways to navigate change in an ever-evolving world. Here are some recommended actions to consider for immediate implementation.[68]

Maintain a schedule. Youth thrive on routines and schedules especially during a pandemic or post-pandemic period. It is vital to find ways to maintain stability of things within our control or range of influence. Routines and schedules are behaviors that increase psychological safety through expected and anticipated actions. Constant unknowns and surprises often increase anxiety and stress because it creates environments of constant change and unknowns.

Decrease exposure to negative news and extreme screen. There are multiple media outlets, digital streams, and talking heads bombarding everyone with opinions and viewpoints. Every news outlet has a different version and agenda on every possible topic in the world. Filtering is imperative and necessary to maintain personal health and wellness.

Humans are social beings with minds, emotions, feelings, and senses that are stimulated by internal and external variables. Naturally, every person responds to stimuli in positive or

---

[67] M.S. Cardon et. al., "Exploring the Heart: Entrepreneurial Emotion is a Hot Topic," *Entrepreneurship Theory and Practice* 36, no. 1 (2021): 1–10.

[68] ContentEngine LLC. trans., "Emotional Intelligence and Social-Emotional Skills for Children's Lives," *CE Noticias Financieras*, 2021.

negative ways, and global media is aware of the intricacies of human behavior. So much so, they often hire behavioral scientists and neurologists to utilize their expertise to control the public through fear, threats, conspiracy theories, doubt, and mistrust in the minds of the public. Fear, doubt, and mistrust fuels the need to defend oneself at all costs from the perceived unknown planted in the public's minds and thoughts. Military coups, uprisings, rebellion, and wars are sometimes fueled by the same concept.

Big media and companies understand the psychological underpinnings of the brain and often use information against their customers, patrons, and followers. The Erikson Theory explains that "every person experiences a psychosocial crisis, which has a positive or negative outcome impacting their personality development."[69] Excessive screen time on any device or unit impacts mental health and wellness over time. Recent studies confirm over usage of digital devices rapidly leads to internet addiction (IA) and Problematic Internet Use (PIU).[70] Also, studies reflect IA among adolescents was strongly related to "worsening psychiatric symptoms, sleeping disturbances, later bedtimes, obesity, and poor academic performance."[71] Therefore, it is imperative to set daily boundaries and filters around exposure to negative news, conversations, and time limits to digital screen exposure.

[69.] Dr. Saul McLeod, "Erik Erikson's Stages of Psychosocial Development," *Simple Psychology*, 2018, https://www.simplypsychology.org/Erik-Erikson.html.
[70.] Hideki Nakayama et. al., "Change of Internet Use and Bedtime Among Junior High School Students After Long-Term School Closure Due to the Coronavirus Disease 2019 Pandemic," *Children Basel* 80, no. 6 (2021): 480.
[71.] Nakayama. et. al., "Change of Internet Use," 480.

Maintain digital wellness. Youth need to limit, filter, and set boundaries around information being received and processed in their minds and brains to support the maintenance of their digital and psychological well-being. It is vital to emphasize mental health during a pandemic, lockdown, and afterward. Several pandemic-related stressors became apparent, and it is essential to pay attention to them.

To maintain digital wellness, it is advisable to have a structured routine, reduce passive screen time, lower exposure to news media about the pandemic, safely spend more time outdoors, and obtain adequate sleep to reduce mental disorders.[72] Increased use of digital devices and apps massively increases data vulnerability to hackers, cyber attackers, and the dark web. Also, online stalking and bullying are threats to the psychological safety of youth and families. Our youth can focus on what is within their control daily by filtering and limiting the flow of information seen, heard, or mentally processed. In addition, they can increase consumption of the positive things in life, including the love of family and friends and activities that increase their joy. Maintaining digital wellness is necessary to robustly increase creativity, imagination, entrepreneurial, and innovative ideas in youth.

Acknowledge fears or anxiety. It is crucial for adults to actively listen to our youth during challenging and uncertain times. Scientists believe anxiety is a result of three factors combined: biological, psychological, and social or a biopsychosocial model.[73]

---

[72] Maya L. Rosen et. al., "Promoting Youth Mental Health during the COVID-19 Pandemic: A Longitudinal Study," 16, no. 8 (2021): 5.

[73] Heather Cameron, "Fear," *Medical Journal of Australia* 213, no. 11 (2020): 525.

Therefore, our youth deserve to be heard and to express their feelings and emotions in words and other artistic mediums such as art, music, poetry, manuscripts, etc. By having space for our youth to express their personal feelings, their anxiety will be reduced.

In addition, leaders are not self-serving; therefore, they are genuinely interested in the well-being of others because their focus is to address others' needs. Leaders want to know more about the challenges and concerns of others, so they can respond and offer support and potential solutions. By always giving others space to express themselves, leaders help them unpack feelings without taking them personally. Instead, leaders are curious and find valuable and insightful ways to offer support.

Promote quality time. Our culture today focuses on embracing quality time. The global pandemic offered the gift of self-reflection, time to reconnect with our purpose, and evaluate alignments. It is important to know the "why" for all we say and do because this understanding increases our ability to live with purpose and intention. All we say and do should benefit, develop, and grow others and not harm them. Quality time provides space to do what is valuable to each person and reach individual and collective goals. Time allows us to live with intention and create legacies that are meaningful to us and others. Also, quality time promotes productivity through time management. Time is spent by everyone, but it is important to focus on the quality of time used and what is yielded from it. Quality time results in improved relationships and a more harmonious life, including an increase in physical movement, establishing family goals, maintaining healthy sleep patterns, and creating a nutrition plan.

Youth leaders have a vision, know their mission, and align with their purpose. They are effective and make impacts. Youth leaders imagine a vision in the future larger and more desirable than what is seen in the present. They possess attitude and confidence, which are two characteristics separating them from a follower. However, effective leaders begin developing their leadership by demonstrating followership first. Leaders know their purpose, and their leadership is set on a firm foundation of belief. They believe in their vision and the significance of what they are called to accomplish. Their accomplishments are not for self-gratification. Their accomplishments are a by-product of fulfilling their purpose, which is shared with the world to benefit the world. Our purpose is always greater than ourselves.

True leaders continuously mature and grow their mindset. They are in a rapid state of growth and learning, so digital wellness and technology is not a hinderance for them. Instead, technology is another tool they use to fulfill their purpose. Leaders move with self-assurance and confidence, keeping fear and anxiety at a distance. Leaders take possession of their territory, protect, and war for it, if necessary. As Scripture states, "What a man thinketh, so is he."[74] Leaders have healthy attitudes, which are a product of their belief. They grow their mind through faith and knowledge, which fuels their awareness and

---

[74.] Prov. 23:7.

intelligence. Their mentality matches their ability to accomplish all things "through Christ who strengthens them."[75]

Leaders know how to incorporate their faith and belief in God in all they do. They are one in Christ and made in "the image of God."[76] While in school or attending to their studies, they bring reinforcements to help them excel. It is a spiritual principle I am thankful to have finally learned, although I would have used it much sooner had I known. While studying anything, leaders know to pray and anoint their books, notebooks, writing instruments, laptops, digital readers, and any tool used to facilitate their work. I was an average student most of my academic journey from grade school to my college undergraduate program. My grade point average (GPA) soared and consistently remained at an A-average through all my graduate degree studies. The most intelligent decision any leader can make is walking and aligning with the power of God.

[75.] Phil. 4:13.
[76.] Gen. 1:27; James 3:9.

5
NAVIGATING THROUGH CONFLICT

We are introduced to conflict early in life, mostly during our infancy stage. Recent research confirms through functional MRI imaging the level of pain and conflict newborn babies experience after birth.[77] The way we deal with conflict largely depends on the stage of our lifecycle, maturity, experience, and development. Conflict arises between people with different thought processes, understanding, interests, and attitudes. Particularly, conflict becomes evident when there are opposing positions between people; therefore, it is often seen as a negative situation. However, there are multiple benefits to conflict, and it is a normal part of life. It will happen and happen often because each person is a unique individual totally unlike the other. Therefore, conflict provides an opportunity

---

77. M. Ranger and R. E. Grunau, "How do babies feel pain?" *ELife*, 4 (2015): https://doi.org/10.7554/eLife.07552.

for individuals to develop skills in negotiation, mediation, arbitration, and litigation. When leaders are in the company of innovative people, it is natural to engage in productive conflict to debate about ideas and strategies; it is called progress.

Leaders can find guidance and examples of conflict resolution multiple times in the Bible. Our first example of how God demonstrates His process of conflict resolution is in the Garden of Eden, and later we see a strong example of conflict resolution through the story of Joseph. In Genesis 3, God created Adam for the purpose of him managing the garden, naming the animals, ruling, and taking dominion. God said it was not good for Adam to be alone, so God created woman. Adam did not give her the name Eve until after the fall of man in Genesis 3:20.

Everything was going well until the woman was tempted by the serpent to do what God commanded Adam not to do. Adam was not to eat from the tree of the knowledge of good and evil for when he eats of it, he "will surely die."[78] After God issued this commandment to Adam, God created woman, Adam's helper. This entire story centers on God's kingdom, order, obedience, and being an imitator of God, The Creator. Since God created Adam first to rule, reign, and take dominion of all creation, it was Adam's responsibility to protect and have authority over the woman. God gave Adam the garden as his domain. Divine kingdom order is the same today as it was at creation. Dysfunction and problems develop when this divine order is not implemented and successfully executed. The divine order places:

[78.] Gen. 2:17.

- God first as Creator
- Man (first Adam) to reign and rule on earth, which is his inheritance
- Woman submitting to a man of God as his helpmate and supporter

After the woman eats the fruit from the tree of the knowledge of good and evil, God walks through the garden in the cool of the day to commune with Adam, His creation. However, Adam and the woman are hiding among the trees of the garden. Note the following narrative and particularly how God coaches them through this conflict and reaches a resolution.

1. God called to the man asking, "where are you?"[79] God is making an inquiry of Adam. Does God know the answer before asking the question? Of course, He does, but He is a loving Father, and a loving parent gives the child an opportunity to speak. God is the Highest Judge and the Great Counselor, as well. Often, we see God defending His law in legal context in the Scriptures by laying out the evidence in full view of His people and prophets. In this context, God begins teaching a lesson of discipline through coaching.

2. Adam answers the question asked by his loving Father by acknowledging he heard Him, but he was afraid. He hid because he was naked.

3. God speaks again like an expert trial attorney and begins to ask a round of skillful coaching questions to His son, Adam. God asks Adam, who told him he was naked?

[79.] Gen. 3:9.

Then God asks Adam if he has eaten from the tree he was commanded to avoid? God is asking direct coaching questions, so His son has an opportunity to repent for his sins. God knows what happened. Through His loving kindness, He pauses and gives him an opportunity to come clean, so he can ask for forgiveness for his wrongdoing and repent. Similarly, God needs_for us to see the truth of our misdeeds. It is only through self-awareness and admission of guilt that will we self-correct and avoid the same sin in the future.

4. Note how Adam responds by avoiding God's first question. Adam never states who told him he was naked. Instead, Adam immediately blames the woman by pointing the finger at her for giving him the fruit from the tree. Adam pitifully continues to defend his case by stating he ate the fruit because she gave it to him. Adam does not repent or ask God for forgiveness. Unlike Adam, effective leaders and rulers do not blame failures on others. They take responsibility and hold themselves accountable for everyone under their authority. True leaders are strong, ethical, and demonstrate integrity. They take the hits and also hold themselves accountable. Leaders take charge of the situation. Let us rewind the tape and look more closely at the evidence. Adam was God's first creation. His purpose and mission was to work and manage the garden, including every creature in it and the woman, who was created to be his helpmate. I doubt the woman was created with a business suit and named Woman CEO. On the contrary, the woman was created to submit to Adam.

5. God turns His attention to the woman to ask her what has she done? Again, God is asking direct coaching questions and giving His children an opportunity to admit their guilt, repent, and ask for forgiveness. Instead, the woman takes a page from Adam's poor defense skills, and she blames the serpent. The woman told God the serpent deceived her, and she ate the fruit. She was left to defend for herself. The man created to protect, love, defend, and provide for her, left her to answer the charges levied upon her and respond to questioning.

6. Next, God turns His attention to the serpent. Obviously, there is no need to ask anything of the serpent, the great deceiver and father of lies, because his response is a standard mode of operation. Since we are imitators of Father God, we should do the same. We should not waste time arguing or negotiating with the deceiver because he has no defense. We should call out, crush the head of the deceiver, and evict him like warriors and rulers. God releases judgment and a sentence upon the serpent, and God's word is final.

7. Then, God turns His attention to the woman. He asks questions regarding her actions, but she has no defense. Her helpmate abandoned her and abdicated his throne, and she failed to admit her sin, repent, or ask God for forgiveness. Therefore, God releases judgment on her regarding pain in childbearing, and she will be ruled by her husband. God addresses them as a marital couple for the first time.

8. Then, God deals with His first-born. Since Adam listened to his wife and ate from the tree, which he was commanded to avoid, God cursed the ground. Now, Adam must labor for his food by the sweat of his brow until he dies and returns to dust. Adam betrayed God, his wife, and himself. Adam failed in his rulership as a leader. He hid himself instead of admitting to sin, repenting, and asking forgiveness from a loving Father, who provided everything he needed and more.

How will we go forward and navigate through conflict resolution differently with our children, family, community, and colleagues? Will we coach through the conflict like the example demonstrated by God in Genesis? Will we share our observances and then pause to ask questions, so we can hear and learn from perspectives other than our own? Differing opinions are great learning opportunities.

Next, we see that Joseph experienced multiple conflicts, and the first one began with his relationship with his brothers, who despised his dreams and boasting. Instead of mentoring Joseph and setting a righteous example of leadership for him, the brothers hated him, threw him in a pit, *continued to eat their lunch*, sold him to traveling merchants for twenty pieces of silver, and told their father Joseph was dead. Conflict can yield one of two things:

- An opportunity to teach, learn, increase a growth mindset, and develop better leaders.
- A pathway to deception, lies, abuse, jealousy, more sin, and harm to self and others.

The initial human conflict with Joseph and his brothers laid a foundation of deception for future events. Conflict resolution in the story of Joseph resulted in deception and hardships for Joseph and his family. After rising in power and becoming the second person in command of Egypt, Joseph did not immediately contact his family about his elevation in social status. The lack of interest in sharing the good news with his family tells a story of its own. Joseph also conceals his identity when he meets his brothers and accuses them of being spies. Joseph's unwillingness to share his accomplishments with his family and to be open and transparent gives us a clear understanding of the family dynamics.

It is unlikely that everyone will agree with one another, which holds the wealth of our learning. Conflict is not unusual; it is an acceptable standard. In life, we witness personal, family, professional, and global conflicts regularly. It is equally important for leaders to ensure conflicts are discussed openly with transparency and not driven underground to bubble in resentment. We are social creatures who require interaction and with increased interactions comes conflict. Therefore, leaders must always prepare themselves for conflict through emotional stability and not take it personally. They are peacemakers deploying patience, self-control, and speaking truth with the love of Jesus Christ.

All leaders can deploy emotional stability by knowing oneself as a mature individual.[80] Emotional stability is described as the predictability and consistency in demonstrating emotional reactions, and the mark of maturity is shown through the

---

80. Engstrom, Christian Leader.

ability to consistently manage one's emotions. Ted Engstrom states, "the way an individual thinks of himself and others greatly determines how he will face tension."[81] Emotional stability is abundantly tested in high-pressure situations and dealing with others' intense situations. Our ability to adjust to change and conflict is largely based on how much we can control. Our ability to successfully adjust is also determined by the value we place on controlling external factors and how much we must compromise or defend our needs.[82] Pressure, chaos, and challenging situations are necessary for us to fully know and understand our authentic selves. Our response to disruptions demonstrates our true intent and nature.

For instance, Joseph faces several incidents of conflict throughout his journey. His first conflict in human relationships was the conflict in behavior and values between him and his older brothers. His brothers held a level of contempt for Joseph that surpasses average sibling rivalry. It was deep-seated and rooted in something evil, sinister, and demonic. Since God said that thoughts convict as well as actions, Joseph's brothers were murderers.[83] Naturally, we would think such evil malice cannot be overcome, especially when we witness maleficence in our workplace, community, and families. However, the love of God overcomes it all, including the most evil intent of the heart.

Therefore, conflicting or opposing opinions and positions are positive occurrences if we change our perspective about them. They are opportunities to explore, discuss, learn, and

[81] Engstrom, *Christian Leader.*
[82] Hutchens, Brain Brilliant.
[83] 1 John 3:20.

grow. This world would be a boring place if everyone continuously had the same thoughts and opinions. There would be little growth, which is one of the problems associated with complacency. Opposing positions allow us to sharpen each other and expand our global mindsets by considering alternative viewpoints. Conflict should not automatically signal a need to prepare for battle or war. It should not be an unwelcome condition or seen from a negative or disruptive viewpoint. Conflict and disruption create pressure or combustion, which is the energy needed to bring forth creative ideas and solutions hidden inside each of us. It is like the enormous amount of pressure needed to transform coal into brilliant, expensive, and multifaceted diamonds.

True leadership is determined by the position and actions of a leader during conflict. Will the leader lean on their understanding when conflict arises, or will the leader lean on God? Faith is the determining factor in discovering new pathways to freedom, and it allows us to stand amid conflict.[84] It is not difficult to proclaim our identity in times of calmness and peace; however, our identity is revealed when the pressure increases, and our potential disruptors are displayed for public viewing.

In addition, James spoke of conflict in the Scriptures. He determined that humans war and experience conflict because of unsatisfied cravings and desires. Conflict arises when a person desires to have their way instead of following the ways of God.[85] Prophet Chuck Pierce posits, *"desire is a function of emotion; emotion is linked with feeling. Conflicts in our emotions can create*

[84.] C. Pierce, R Heidler, and L. Heidler, *A Time to Advance: Understanding the Significance of the Hebrew Tribes and Months* (Denton, T.X.: Zion International, 1982).
[85.] James 4:1-3 (NKJV).

war within us and in the earth around us. This conflict can be individual, territorial, national, or international."[86] In addition, the way leaders handle conflict will determine the type of fruit they bear.

When leaders avoid conflict and debates, they miss opportunities to grow and to develop others into better leaders. There are multiple advantages in welcoming conflict and creative friction. Conflict is not meant to be a fearful, uncomfortable, paralyzing, or distressing process, although it demands attentiveness, time, and energy. The avoidance of conflict benefits no one. However, leaders work to manage discussions until a harmonious resolution is reached, and they ensure that no one takes it personally.[87] Although, conflicts arise from the war within, requiring attention until it is resolved.

Creative friction occurs when opposing ideas and opinions are in direct competition or conflict with one another.[88] However, breakthroughs and resolutions can be reached when leaders shift from creative friction to productive friction. Productive friction is the fertile field full of seeds of growth in unknown or lesser-known areas of knowledge. All humans should be in a perpetual state of learning and growing. Knowledge and information are like the lifecycle of plant life because it fertilizes, aids seed dispersal, germinates, and stimulates the growth of our blooms. Each person should blossom continuously by gaining new or revelatory information from others. The world truly needs more blooms full of knowledge and wisdom.

[86.] C. Pierce, Redeeming The Time: Get Your Life Back on Track with the God of Second Opportunities (New York, N.Y.: Penguin Random House, 2021).

[87.] Gary Oster, *The Light Prize: Perspectives on Christian Innovation* (Virginia Beach: Positive Signs Media, 2011).

[88.] Oster, *Light Prize*.

Conflict can be combative or an opportunity to learn, grow, and thrive. In either case, basic foundational principles are aiding the resolution of opposing positions, so let's review them. We must first ensure that we understand what is being said or shared with clarity in the intent it is given. The goal is to minimize or eliminate any opposition before participants can open the space for exploration through conversation. Through paraphrasing and mirroring back to the speaker, other participants can gain clarity and confirm they heard the speaker accurately. This makes space for the exploration. Ultimately, conflict encourages intentional pauses for observation, listening, growing, and sharing of information.

6
NEGOTIATION & BARGAINING SKILLS

egotiation and bargaining are a natural part of our lives as much as breathing. Infant babies bargain and negotiate with new parents without a bargaining table, and it is not a win-win situation during the early years. The skills acquired in the relationship continue until the relationship ends. As our relationships mature, we begin to understand the importance of prioritizing our top needs and wants, determining what will be our deal-breaker, and figuring out how much to offer others to meet their expectations. The mental, psychological, hierarchical, and emotional bargaining takes place over negotiations.

The concept of negotiation is nothing new. As a matter of fact, the Bible explains the reason for it. The Scriptures explain that quarrels and fights among us derive from the passions that are at war within us.[89] In Genesis, Abraham negotiated with the angels or messengers from heaven; he tried to advocate on

---

89. James 4:1-2.

behalf of the righteous citizens in Sodom and Gomorrah, who would be killed with the wicked when the city was destroyed. Abraham negotiated with the angelic messengers because Abraham was warring with the compassion in his heart for God's righteous people.

Negotiation strategies vary in size and severity based on the stakeholders, persons of interest, and the level of trust or distrust among them. While negotiating, we must remind ourselves there is more than one way to reach a destination or desired end. We can all reach the desired destination, but we will not all take the same pathway; therefore, we must remain open to other ideas and perspectives. It should not feel like we always have the best plan.

Negotiation is a process of resolving disputes and conflicts through effective communication and discussions.[90] Successful negotiation techniques are the result of clear expectations and the investment made in building relationships. The best strategy is knowing how to set clear and consistent objectives. We should negotiate as close as possible to the agreed upon expectation based on its importance. Also, it is important to know what others value, to possess a greater understanding of how they think, and to know the drivers behind their underlying thoughts. We should make every attempt to listen and meet the needs of others when it is beneficial for the common good of everyone, not focus on self-serving initiatives. Instead, we must consider the costs and investment of time, labor, mental

---

[90.] Stephen Denning, The Secret Language of Leadership: How Leaders Inspire Action Through Narrative (San Francisco: Jossey-Bass, 2007).

attention, materials, and resources to determine the best out-come for short-term and long-term benefits.

Both active listening and communicating with clarity are key elements in negotiations and conversations. Some techniques in active listening include maintaining an open mind and build-ing rapport to influence others. During negotiations, patience is the best skill to deploy. The purpose of negotiations is to build bridges across differences, cultures, and misconceptions. Lead-ers deploy this tool to build up families and communities, solve problems, manage conflicts, and preserve relationships.

Attentive listening and effective communication may ap-pear complicated, but much is obtained by listening. Attentive listening allows leaders to determine what is most important to others, and the level of importance. Effective leaders are atten-tive and great observers of actions. They research information about the character of the negotiation partner: who they are at the core, what drives them, what is their experience, and who and what impacts them the most? It is like studying the tape of the opposing team to learn their plays. Leaders study how they speak, what they often say, what inspires them, and what mo-tivates them. People often display their identity and share im-portant information in conversations, interviews, news articles, and public appearances. It is vital to listen attentively to what they do not disclose as much as what they disclose. Leaders watch, observe, and listen to others to identify their internal motives and core values. They consider the brand and reputa-tion of stakeholders to levy an advantage in negotiations, so leaders can regurgitate information their stakeholders consider valuable to them.

Effective negotiations are needed when discussing opposing opinions at the table and within your own group or camp. The healthiest of relationships need negotiation, such as social organizations, marriages, families, and businesses. The leader-follower relationship requires a re-negotiation occasionally because individuals are maturing, growing, and evolving in their thoughts and opinions based on new or updated information. Stakeholders must also understand the newest needs to be met for a balanced negotiation to be successful.[91]

Negotiation and bargaining are delicate relational conversations we initiate with family and business stakeholders. Leaders cannot afford to navigate successfully through negotiation and bargaining based on trust alone. Who should leaders trust, and how much should they trust them? History reflects our complicated relationship with the concept of trust. Negotiating and advising requires leaders to consider the intention to trust, interpersonal trust, and behavioral trust.[92] Each comes with a different level and psychological foundation of trust, which leaders must carefully validate such as past reputation, current actions and behavior, and the emotional value of the relationship.

Young leaders intuitively know how to negotiate without fear. Through their ability to make greater impacts for others' benefit, they know which issues are time-sensitive and appropriate to place on the negotiation table to reach a timely resolution. They are bold and courageous enough to identify

---

91. Chaleff, The Courageous Follower.
92. Julia K. de Groote and Alexandra Bertschi-Michel, "From Intention to Trust to Behavioral Trust: Trust Building in *Family Business* Advising," *Family Business Review* 34, no. 2 (2021): 132-153.

problems and readily come forward with potential solutions. They are candid and transparent in sharing their viewpoints; their perspectives remind adults of future implications if changes are not implemented in a timely manner. Most of all, young leaders are not afraid to ask for what they need.

In addition, youth often have several proposals to pitch when attempting to reach a resolution. Creating multiple strategies before discussions is a recommended approach. Parents are familiar with negotiating with children and their creative proposals to influence a parent to purchase something for them. I remember when my son was younger and pitched a proposal when I had no cash in my wallet. He simply suggested I go to the silver machine that dispensed money whenever someone needed it. He was too young to understand the banking system or how the automated teller machine (ATM) worked. My son's primary goal was to reach his objective and find ways to help his mother make a purchase by using his skills of innovative thinking, honesty, and transparency. My son was exploring creative alternatives and felt psychologically safe to discuss his thoughts and pitch his proposal. All young leaders need space to accomplish the same.

It is vital for young leaders to be observant, attentively listen to mentors and leaders, and feed and nourish their networks by creating allies. By creating diverse networks consisting of creative, innovative, and ethical leaders, young leaders will gain wisdom and be inspired by those who are focused and committed to reach success in their chosen field. Young leaders should meet with others who are further along their leadership journey, so they can glean best practices, wisdom, and information from others. By building key alliances, leader's gain support and the ability to reach workable solutions to the most complex problems and create sustainable collaborations. In contrast, leaders will not accomplish much or globally compete in business, if they spend time trolling social networks, tracking social events, gaming, and hosting idle conversations with friends and others. Successful entrepreneurs and business leaders invest time in building impactful networks, researching, and growing their mindset. There is no need to keep up with others who are not going anywhere fast. Rather, leaders set better examples and leave room for others to fulfill their purpose and mission.

7
YOUR WORK VS. YOUR JOB

The world operates on rules, policies, legislation, culture, and business principles. Yet, some adult leaders are not sure who they are or what they should be doing. If older adults are faced with such inquiries, we can imagine younger leaders having the same inquiries. Most of us agree that adult and youth business leaders should be ethical, moral, and responsible stewards of all resources as they labor in their calling and vocation, but what is a vocation? A vocation is not the sole decision of a leader; rather, it is what a leader has been called to do by God.[93] Christian leaders and entrepreneurs should view a calling as a transition "out of darkness to love God and neighbor."[94] In addition, a vocation is the manner that leaders feel led to fulfill the Great Commission.[95] The Great Commission in Matthew

---

[93.] Ben III. Witherington, *Work – A Kingdom Perspective*, (Grand Rapids: Wm. B. Eerdmans Publishing Co., 2011), 31.
[94.] Witherington, 32.
[95.] Witherington, 32.

28:19 states all people are to spread the Gospel of Jesus Christ and "make disciples of all the nations."

The apostle Paul reminds leaders and entrepreneurs to be co-laborers with God because there is a "mutual dependence between God and human beings in the task of preservation of creation."[96] Many leaders proclaim to be self-made, but is that true? The full meaning of being self-made is to create yourself and sustain yourself with no assistance, support, or help from anyone at any point in your life's journey. Based on this definition, most people do not qualify for this category.

Also, the leaders' personality and interpersonal skills should align with their divine assignment.[97] Gary Oster posits, "leaders respond to the call to listen to and mimic God by creating works that show our honor and adoration."[98] We are created in God's image; therefore, we find our purpose and reason for our design by communing with the One who created us. Each of us is created for a specific purpose, and it is our job to discover what it is and execute our assignment. God authorizes leaders and empowers them to do good works on the earth as a reflection of His image. We are God's "personal agents, who are empowered by the Almighty."[99] We do not accomplish much when we are self-empowered and self-dependent.

Furthermore, much of the world yearns to experience the American culture marketed as the land of milk and honey. Information about America and what it offers is often based

---

96. Witherington, 32.
97. Witherington, 35.
98. Oster, *Light Prize*, 66.
99. Witherington, 29.

on half-truths regarding opportunities, prosperity, and wealth. America has opportunities for people who leverage their muscles of resiliency, determination, business acumen, strategy, and prayer. However, the world seldom sees the gulches of poverty, child hunger, and other society shortfalls in America due to oppression, abuse, and inequality. Is America the only location for opportunities, prosperity, wealth, and success? Absolutely not! God's laws work wherever we are without geographical restriction; however, how we apply God's laws will determine the outcome.

Success, prosperity, peace, and joy are not geographical locations. The Holy Bible reflects God's formula for success, which is not restricted by geographical location. God was not born in America; therefore, success can be obtained anywhere God is accepted in the heart of man, and man walks in obedience to the laws, covenants, and ordinances of God. Joshua 1:8 states, *"This Book of the Law shall not depart from your mouth, but you shall meditate in it day and night, that you may observe to do according to all that is written in it. For then you will make your way prosperous, and then you will have good success."* Also, Matthew 6:33 states, "but seek first the kingdom of God and His righteousness, and all these things shall be added to you." These two Scriptures do not restrict the blessings of God to any geographical location, person, ethnic group, or country.

The biblical principles relating to work and what God designed man to do are the key to understanding success and its alignment to our purpose. Unfortunately, the American education system does not teach principles aligned with the purpose of our creation. Instead, the American culture teaches and emphasizes the need to obtain an education to secure a job. God's purpose is for man to work, but it is important to understand work is not the same as a job.

In the first chapter of the Book of Genesis, God created for six days and rested on the seventh. God worked to design everything and saw that "it was good."[100] On the sixth day, God created Adam and commanded him to work. Adam's first job was to name all the animals and to tend to the Garden of Eden. Adam was working before God created Eve; therefore, man should work as responsible providers before seeking a wife and helpmate. Adam did not ask God's assistance to fashion a resume and give him a business suit, so he could seek a job. Adam was created for the work he was assigned to do, and the same applies to each human being. God created each of us with a set of gifts to deploy for the building of the Kingdom of God. Proverbs 18:16 also states, "a man's gift makes room for him and brings him before great men." Our work is tied to our purpose, and work allows us to be deployed in service to God. We cannot be fired, hired, laid off, or resign from our work. For example, birds are designed to use their wings to fly; therefore, their wings are part of their purpose and allow them to perform their work. Birds do not tire of flying and retire from it. Incidentally, many birds migrate thousands of miles each year for breeding and feeding. Birds will fly until they are unable to do so or die. Man is designed to work until the last breath is taken. Man should not retire from what he is created and designed to do because man's work is tied to his success, purpose, and prosperity.

[100.] Gen. 1:31.

Man must work, so he can execute the commands of God. However, work has nothing to do with finding a job. Work is becoming who you are. A bird is designed to fly and that is his work. When a seed produces a plant or a tree, it is doing its work or fulfilling its purpose. Work allows people to become who they are. Work gives man an opportunity to participate in the good deeds of God because everything God created was good. Most definitions of work allude to the ability to labor for the sake of sustaining and surviving. However, Quinn and Strickland explain that work "is what creatures do with God's creation."[101] If we believe work is only for the means of sustaining and surviving, then we should not be surprised when a worker has deteriorating health, contracts disease, falls ill, and dies at an early age. In addition, Frederick Buechner's definition of work states it is "the place where your deep gladness meets the world's deep need."[102] In other words, work can be found at the intersection of joy and need. Our greatest reward is knowing we are doing something purposeful to support and enhance the lives of others.

Jobs are created for the benefit of the business owner or employer. The employer decides who to hire, fire, lay-off, promote, demote, and force into mandatory retirement. However, there are multiple benefits associated with jobs. Jobs are designed to be temporary training grounds with a limited shelf life. Jobs allow people to receive compensation, benefits, free skills, and training to use for the deployment of their work. Often, workers become disgruntled, disengaged, and angry when they

---

[101.] B. Quinn and W. II. Strickland, *Every Waking Hour: An Introduction to Work and Vocation for Christians*, (Bellingham, W.A.: Lexham Press, 2016).

[102.] Frederick Buechner, *Wishful Thinking: A Seeker's ABC* (San Francisco: Harper, 1993).

remain with an employer too long instead of leaving the job to be deployed to perform their work. Regardless, jobs employ and compensate workers based on an opinion of what the workers' labor is worth. However, man cannot be reduced to his individual labor, and no one else can truly assess his value or worth.[103]

103. Witherington, Kingdom Perspective.

8
BE FRUITFUL AND MULTIPLY

Work affords entrepreneurs and leaders opportunities to build wealth, increase the fruits of their labor, and multiply what they sow. A survey by Inc. Magazine revealed 47 percent of business opportunity discoveries arise from work activity.[104] Work is the foundation that leads to the path of discovering new business opportunities; these opportunities allow leaders to match a market with a specific product or service and revenue potential.[105] Work increases our mental stamina, gives us purpose, and provides an opportunity to develop, train, and assist others. Through work, we gain a deeper understanding of God, our Creator. Colossians 1:10 states, "[we] walk worthy of the Lord unto all pleasing, being fruitful in every good work and increasing in the knowledge of God."[106]

---

104. Karl H. Vesper, *New Venture Mechanics* (Englewood Cliffs, New Jersey: Prentice Hall), 1.
105. Vesper, 5.
106. Colossians 1:10 (KJV).

Fruitfulness involves coming into the fullness or full bloom of ourselves and multiplying our whole self. Every plant, fruit, or vegetable yield blooms before the natural growth cycle of it producing food for us. In some instances, the bloom and the food item are edible; therefore, the plant has increased or multiplied what it is able to produce. Fruitfulness is linked with prosperity in the war of poverty.

The disciples and followers of Christ sacrificed, and in some instances, they gave away their belongings and possessions. Early in Jesus' ministry, He hand-selected disciples to follow Him to spread the Good News of the Gospel. Jesus told the disciples to sell their possessions, give to the poor, and follow Him.[107] Jesus asked His followers to deny themselves, cast down their idols (love of money, self-righteousness, vanity, and pride), and follow Him; with Him, they will lack nothing. They traveled and spread the Gospel with little in their possession because God provided for their needs. They did not have to beg, borrow, or steal to satisfy their material or spiritual needs. They were hosted at others 'homes, offered prepared meals and bread, money, and a place to recline for the night.[108]

Trapped within every leader is a seed, and it is the responsibility of the leader to unlock it! Unlocking the seed unlocks inner strength, vision, and purpose. When young leaders are in a healthy ecosystem where they can develop and thrive, their potential is unlimited. They become like a forest of strong, vibrant trees

---

107. Mark 10:21; Matthew 19:21; Luke 18:22.
108. Mark 6:10; Luke 9:4; Luke 10:5; Luke 10:38-42.

with branches reaching the sky. Their vision, creativity, and innovative thinking has no bounds. Leadership involves strong mindsets, visions, and confidence.

We want our youth to be multiple forests or huge redwoods and oaks that will weather every storm and obstacle. The nutrients needed to feed the tree are entered through the root system. What are we feeding our youth? Are we feeding them knowledge, business, and life skills to establish a firm foundation of entrepreneurship, or are we planting seeds that bloom into finding a job, working for thirty years, and retiring? If so, we are encouraging them to build wealth for others, so they can eventually come home and scrape out a living on a pension, unable to keep pace with living costs and taxes. I pray we have a greater vision for them than this.

Vision allows others to see life differently. For example, most people do not bother to pick up a penny when it drops from their pocket or purse in the parking lot. If we look at the penny at face value, it is only worth one cent. However, if we retrieve the penny, add it to other pennies, and invest it, we can multiple the penny to produce dollars. The penny is a seed capable of producing huge oak trees. When we see a forest of trees, do we see a furniture piece it can become? When we see a flower bloom, do we taste a menu item at an expensive restaurant? Vision allows us to see the possibilities and improve the world around us.

Young leaders must be careful not to corrupt, pollute, or threaten the growth of their seed by listening or viewing anything toxic for fear of corrupting their mind and spirit. There are volumes of social distractions aimed at polluting the strength of our youth. Nearly everything is threatening the growth and development of our youth in our toxic society. Corruption of any kind leads to various levels of depression, mental impairment, and potentially suicide.

However, fruitfulness results from living with the boundaries of blessing that yield prosperity, security, joy, abundance, protection, health, and satisfaction.[109] Through work, we earn compensation and gain a deeper understanding of God. Colossians 1:10 states, "[we] walk worthy of the Lord unto all pleasing, being fruitful in every good work and increasing in the knowledge of God."[110] However, to create and sustain wealth for the pleasure of the Lord, God requires us to tithe and bring offerings into the storehouse, so He can multiply them.[111] God multiplies everything He touches and increases yields. We offer our first fruits to Him in the form of tithes and offerings, so there will always be meat in His house or enough to distribute and share with others in need.[112] Our provision is secured through our giving and caring of others.

Work results in multiple benefits for us. It also creates the potential for wealth-building because wealth is the result of enterprise and useful work.[113] Wealth offers an opportunity to invest in others and support the prosperity of others. Wealth represents more than money or capital. Wealth can be generated by "asking obviously stupid questions and exaggerating

---

[109.] C. Pierce and R. Heidler, *A Time to Prosper: Finding and Entering God's Realm of Blessings* (Bloomington, MN: Chosen Books, 2013), 66.

[110.] Col. 1:10.

[111.] Gen. 22:17.

[112.] Mal. 3:10.

[113.] Pierce and Heidler, *Time to Prosper*, 177.

what is new, small, and universally considered irrelevant."[114] Money facilitates transactions and allows the purchase and sale of goods; its value is determined by the trading partners' belief that it has value.[115] Jay Richards posits, "only the creation of wealth will reduce poverty" and allow others to sustain prosperity.[116]

Youth should not be excluded from potential wealth-building around the world. Fortunately, international educational organizations are launching each year to fill the gap of opportunities between American youth from those who are not English-speaking and live in third-world or war-torn countries. For instance, small business incubators for refugee teens launched by the non-profit organization, *Hello Future*, lifts teens from refugee camps in Iraqi Kurdistan into stable, self-reliant opportunities.[117] *Hello Future* also designed a condensed Master of Business Administration (MBA) program with "portable, transferable knowledge" to withstand changes in market conditions despite the geographic location of the refugee student.[118] Youth learn from case studies and are offered mentorship opportunities with business leaders. Upon graduation, each student is awarded a small grant to launch a start-up business. *Global Changemakers* is another international youth organization supporting youth-led sustainable development in 180 countries through mentoring, grants, and the building of

---

114. Oster, *Light Prize*, 1765.
115. Jay W. Richards, *Money, Greed, and God* (New York: HarperOne, 2010), 94.
116. Richards, *Money, Greed*, 8.
117. "Hello Future Set to Launch Small Business Incubator for Refugee Youth," *PR Newswire*, April 12th, 2021, https://www.prnewswire.com/news-releases/hello-future-set-to-launch-small-business-incubator-for-refugee-youth-301266595.html.
118. *PR Newswire*, "Hello Future."

skills.[119] Other youth development programs and incubators internationally include:

- *Nigerian Youth Initiative (NYI)*, an international non-profit working to improve youth skill development in Nigeria.[120]

- *International Youth Foundation (IYF)*, a non-profit focused on supporting youth for 30 years through youth agency, economic opportunity, and systems change.[121]

- *United Nations Environment Program (UNEP)*, a global authority promoting the coherent implementation of the environmental dimension of sustainable development within the United Nations system and setting an environmental agenda.[122]

- *Usher's New Look (UNL)*, a 10-year leadership program developing under-resourced youth through multiple leadership certifications launched by eight-time Grammy award-winning R&B artist, Usher Raymond.[123]

- *Sports Leadership and Management (SLAM)*, a public charter school for disadvantaged youth grades 6-12 funded by Armando Christian Pérez or Grammy-awarding winner rapper, Pitbull. He also funds many youth initiatives in Miami that he founded.[124]

---

[119]. "Empower Youth and Make a Difference," Global Changemakers, last modified 2021, https://www.global-changemakers.net/.

[120]. Nigerian Youths Initiatives, "About," Facebook, https://www.facebook.com/NYI.ORG.NG/.

[121]. "Who We Are," International Youth Foundation, last modified 2021, https://iyfglobal.org/.

[122]. "In Focus," UN Environment Programme, https://www.unep.org/.

[123]. "Transforming Teens Who Change the World," Usher's New Look, August 27th, 2021, https://ushersnewlook.org/.

[124]. "Mission and Vision," Slam: Sports Leadership and Management, https://www.slam-miami.com/.

Historically, wealth and poverty have been misrepresented and used as a divisive paradigm to exploit the less fortunate. Richards posit, "although we link wealth with material possessions -with stuff- the essence of wealth, even though it involves matter, is immaterial. Wealth is not about stuff; it is about us."[125] Each person is a steward of their possessions, including how they are to be utilized and shared. God encourages Christians to possess and protect their inheritance and leave a portion of their harvest or wealth for others so that they can eat and prosper.[126] It is God's intent for us all to prosper through Him.

Leaders, business owners, and the public feel purchasing insurance and maintenance policies are the only way to protect inheritances and possessions. Yet, various types of policies are not guaranteeing a person will be covered because those documents have multiple caveats, restrictions, and limitations regarding specific circumstances. However, our loving Father gives us a 100% guarantee for every promise He has given us. It is the best policy available, and it has been paid in full through the blood of Jesus Christ. Unfortunately, I think many people forget it is available, or they are not aware how to apply and use it.

The full coverage policy from the kingdom is called offerings and tithes. It is specifically mentioned in Malachi 3:10, and its benefits are covered between Genesis and Revelation. Tithing and offerings is how I cover myself, my family, and my businesses (workplace ministries) because everything I do should be like an act of worship to God. Through my tithes, offerings,

---

[125.] Richards, *Money, Greed*, 93.
[126.] Lev. 23:22.

and obedience, God multiplies my finances, blessings, healings, spiritual gifts, and all I do.

There are multiple ways to apply His full coverage policy, and I will share a few for your consideration. When I paint walls in my home, I place a drop of anointing oil in the paint can and pray over the paint before beginning my paint project. When I replace flooring in my home, I write Scripture verses on the sub-floor, anoint, and bless the floors before I allow the contractors to complete the project. I walk my property, sprinkle anointing oil, and speak in my Heavenly Father's language, which is tongues, blessing and protecting my property. I am ruling and reining as I take possession of my property. I am blessing, anointing, and committing my dwelling to the Lord because He provided it to me. Every good thing comes from the Lord.[127] I am taking full possession of my inheritance from my Heavenly Father.

God commanded us to rule and reign everywhere we go. When traveling, the first thing I do when I enter the hotel room is pray and bless the room and the beds with anointing oil. I pray and anoint my office space and conference rooms every week and before contentious meetings to ensure His Presence would be in our midst. Those were some of my most productive meetings. Leaders are always fruitful, and they multiply everywhere. They replicate and duplicate the Holy Spirit in them to others. It is possible to multiply our image of God when we release ourselves from the bondage and traditional thinking of only communing with God on Sundays and bible

---

[127.] James 1:17-18.

study nights. We should never place Him on the shelf. I always carry anointing oil with me, so I can anoint and heal others. Sometimes, it is necessary to anoint myself before executing an assignment by God. Leaders are warriors, and we remain armed with a victorious arsenal. We should always have the right tools for the work, and we cannot go to work empty-handed. Leaders always remain ready for divine deployment. We should exercise our faith day and night by communing with a 24/7 Father and His Son, Jesus. By teaching our youth leaders to commune constantly with the Father, we set them up to flourish as leaders and build the kingdom of God.

BIBLIOGRAPHY

Allen, Jared S., Regan M. Stevenson, Ernest H. O'Boyle, and Scott Seibert. "What Matters More for Entrepreneurship Success? A meta-analysis Comparing General Mental Ability and Emotional Intelligence in Entrepreneurial Settings," *Strategic Entrepreneurship Journal* 15, no. 3 (2021): 352-376.

Allen-Handy, Ayana, Shawnna L. Thomas-El, and Kenzo K. Sung. "Urban Youth Scholars: Cultivating Critical Global Leadership Development through Youth-Led Justice-Oriented Research," *The Urban Review* 53 (2020): 270.

Anwer, Moazama Iqbal Malik Najma, Aneela Maqsood, and Ghazala Rehman. "The Moderating Role of Social Intelligence in Explaining Attachment Style and Emotional Intelligence Among Young Adults," *Pakistan Journal of Psychology* 48, no. 2 (2017): 1-19.

Brothers, Chambers. *Language and Pursuit of Leadership Excellence.* Naples, F.L.: New Possibilities Press, 2015.

Buechner, Frederick. *Wishful Thinking: A Seeker's ABC*. San Francisco: Harper, 1993.

Cameron, Heather. "Fear," *Medical Journal of Australia* 213, no. 11 (2020): 525.

Canton, James. *Future Smart: Managing the Game-Changing Trends That Will Transform Your World*. Philadelphia: Da Capo Press, 2016.

Cardon, M.S., M. D. Foo, D. Shepherd, & J. Wiklund, "Exploring the Heart: Entrepreneurial Emotion is a Hot Topic," *Entrepreneurship Theory and Practice* 36, no. 1 (2021): 1–10.

Chaleff, Ira. *The Courageous Follower: Standing Up to & for our Leaders 2 ed*. San Francisco: Berrett-Koehler, 2003.

ContentEngine LLC., trans. "Emotional Intelligence and Social-Emotional Skills for Children's Lives." *CE Noticias Financieras*, 2021.

Cook, Catherine and Sandy Fertman Ryan. "I Became a Millionaire at 17!" *Girls' Life* 15, no. 6 (2009): 82.

De Groote, Julia K. and Alexandra Bertschi-Michel. "From Intention to Trust to Behavioral Trust: Trust Building in Family Business Advising." *Family Business Review* 34, no. 2 (2021): 132-153.

Denning, Stephen. *The Secret Language of Leadership: How Leaders Inspire Action Through Narrative*. San Francisco: Jossey-Bass, 2007.

Donne, John. "No Man is an Island" [Title Derived]. Wakefield Express, 2021.

Edelman, Andrea, P. Gill, K. Comerford, K. Larson, and R. Hare. "Youth development and Youth leadership: A Background Paper." National Collaborative on Workforce and Disability for Youth (June 2004): 4.

Engstrom, Ted W. *The Making of a Christian Leader*. Grand Rapids: Zondervan, 1976.

Forbes. "Forbes Profile: Grace Beverley." Last modified 2021. https://www.forbes.com/profile/gracebeverley/?sh=a0fda8bd8a4e.

Global Changemakers. "Empower Youth and Make a Difference." Last modified 2021, https://www.global-changemakers.net/.

Greenleaf, Robert. *Servant Leadership: A Journey Into the Nature of Legitimate Power and Greatness*. NewYork: Paulist Press, 2002.

Hashmi, Fatima, Aftab Hira, José Moleiro Martins, Mário Nuno Mata, Hamza Ahmad Qureshi, António Abreu, and Pedro Neves Mata. "The Role of Self-Esteem, Optimism, Deliberative Thinking and Self-Control in Shaping the Financial Behavior and Financial Well-being of Young Adults," *PloS One* 16, no. 9 (2021): 1-23.

Hutchens, Amy K. *Brain Brilliant: Increase Your Personal and Professional Profit*. Atlanta: Amy K. Publishing, 2002.

International Youth Foundation. "Who We Are." Last modified 2021, https://iyfglobal.org/.

Kaplan, Steven N. and Morten Sorensen. "Are CEOs Different?" *The Journal of Finance* 76, no. 4 (2021): 1773.

Kelley, R.E. *The Power of Followership: How to Create Leaders People Want to Follow*. New York, N.Y.: Doubleday, 1992.

Knackendoffel, .Ann E. "Collaborative Teaming in the Secondary School," *Focus on Exceptional Children* 40, no 4 (2007): 1-20.

Larsson, Magnus and Mie Femø Nielsen. "The Risky Path to a Followership Identity: From Abstract Concept to Situated Reality," *International Journal of Business Communication* 58, no. 1 (2017): 3-30.

Lemelson-MIT Program. "US Teens Confident in their Inventiveness; Hands-on, Project-Based Learning Needed," January 17th, 2008, sciencedaily.com.

Lyons, Justin D. *Alexander the Great and Hernán Cortés: Ambiguous Legacies of Leadership.* Blue Ridge Summit: Lexington Books, 2015.

Mathieu, J.E. , J.R. Hollenbeck, D. van Knippenberg, and D.R. Ilgen. "A Century of Work Teams," *Journal of Applied Psychology* 102, no. 3 (2017): 452-467.

McLeod, Dr. Saul. "Erik Erikson's Stages of Psychosocial Development." *Simple Psychology*, 2018, https://www.simplypsychology.org/Erik-Erikson.html.

Molinaro, Vince. *Accountable Leaders: Inspire a Culture Where Everyone Steps Up, Takes Ownership, and Deliver Results.* Gildan Media, 2020.

Monroy, Claire, Chen Chi-Hsin, Derek Houston, .and Chen Yu. "Action Prediction During Real-Time Parent-Infant Interactions." *Developmental Science* (2021): 1-12.

Mr. Cory's Cookies. "Our Story." Last modified 2021. https://mrcoryscookies.com/pages/our-story.

Munroe, Myles. *The Spirit of Leadership: Cultivating the Attributes that Influence Human Action.* New Kensington, P.A. Whitaker House, 2018.

Nakayama, Hideki, Takanobu Matsuzaki, Satoko Mihara, Takashi Kitayuguchi, and Susumu Higuchi. "Change of Internet Use and Bedtime Among Junior High School Students After

Long-Term School Closure Due to the Coronavirus Disease 2019 Pandemic," *Children Basel* 80, no. 6 (2021): 480.

Nigerian Youths Initiatives. "About." Facebook, https://www.facebook.com/NYI.ORG.NG/.

Nobel Peace Prize Foundation. "Malala Yousafzai Biographical." Last modified 2014. https://www.nobelprize.org/prizes/peace-/2014/yousafzai/biographical/.

Northouse, P.G. *Leadership: Theory and practice 6th ed.* Thousand Oaks: SAGE, 2019.

Oster, Gary. *The Light Prize: Perspectives on Christian Innovation.* Virginia Beach: Positive Signs Media, 2011.

Peyton, Nellie. "Generation COVID: How the Young are Working Round Pandemic-hit Job Market," *Reuters*, January 11, 2021, https://www.reuters.com/article/health-coronavirus-youth-employment/generation-covid-how-the-young-are-working-round-pandemic-hit-job-market.

Pierce, C. *Redeeming The Time: Get Your Life Back on Track with the God of Second Opportunities.* New York, N.Y.: Penguin Random House, 2021.

Pierce, C. and R. Heidler. *A Time to Prosper: Finding and Entering God's Realm of Blessings.* Bloomington, MN: Chosen Books, 2013.

Pierce, C., R Heidler, and L. Heidler, *A Time to Advance: Understanding the Significance of the Hebrew Tribes and Months.* Denton, T.X.: Zion International, 1982.

PR Newswire. "Hello Future Set to Launch Small Business Incubator for Refugee Youth," April 12th, 2021, https://www.prnewswire.com/news-releases/hello-future-set-to-launch-small-business-incubator-for-refugee-youth-301266595.html.

---. "Teen Entrepreneur Wins Big: 15-Year-Old Founder of Online E-Reuse Business Named Next Teen Tycoon by VerticalResponse: Three Winning Teens Receive Prizes Worth $10,000 to Grow their Businesses," March 22nd, 2012, https://www.prnewswire.com/news-releases/teen-entrepreneur-wins-big-15-year-old-founder-of-online-e-reuse-business-named-next-teen-tycoon-by-verticalresponse-143801496.html.

Quinn, B. and W. II. Strickland. *Every Waking Hour: An Introduction to Work and Vocation for Christians*. Bellingham, W.A.: Lexham Press, 2016.

Ranger, M. and R. E. Grunau. "How do babies feel pain?" *ELife*, 4 (2015): https://doi.org/10.7554/eLife.07552.

Ratcliffe, John. "Property futures—the Art and Science of Strategic Foresight," *Journal of Property Investment & Finance* 38 (5 (2020): 483-498.

Reese, Simon R. "Implement Strategic Foresight with Elements of the US army's Operational Art Model." *Strategic Direction* 36, no. 5 (2020): 5-8.

Renzulli, Kerri Anne. "Here are the 15 Job Disappearing the Fastest in the U.S." *CNBC*, April 28, 2019, https://www.cnbc.com/2019/04/26/the-15-us-jobs-disappearing-the-fastest.html.

Richards, Jay W. *Money, Greed, and God*. New York: HarperOne, 2010.

Riggio, Ronald E. and Rebecca J. Reichard. "The Emotional and Social Intelligences of Effective Leadership: An Emotional and Social Skill Approach," *Journal of Managerial Psychology* 23, no. 2 (2008): 169-185.

Rosen, Maya L., Alexandra M. Rodman, Steven W. Kasparek, Makeda Mayes, Malila M. Freeman, Liliana J. Lengua, Andrew N. Meltzoff, and Katie A. McLaughli. "Promoting Youth Mental Health during the COVID-19 Pandemic: A Longitudinal Study," 16, no. 8 (2021): 3-5.

Slam: Sports Leadership and Management. "Mission and Vision." https://www.slammiami.com/.

Solar Sister. "Greta Thunberg Foundation Donates to People Fighting the Climate Crisis in Africa." September 23rd, 2020. https://solarsister.org/greta-thunberg-foundation-donates-to-people-fighting-the-climate-crisis-in-africa/.

Time. "Meet Time's First Ever Kid of the year." December 3, 2020. https://time.com/5916772/kid-of-the-year-2020/.

Youth Business International. "Impact Report 2020." Last modified 2021. https://impact2020.youthbusiness.org/.

Youth Market Alerts. "Teens Confident They Will Land Dream Jobs," 22, no. 6 (2010): 8.

Usher's New Look. "Transforming Teens Who Change the World." August 27th, 2021, https://ushersnewlook.org/.

UN Environment Programme. "In Focus." https://www.unep.org/.

Van Linden, J. A. and C. I. Fertman. "Youth Leadership: A Guide to Understanding Leadership Development in Adolescents." *Adolescence* 33, no. 131 (Fall 1998): 720.

Vesper, Karl H. *New Venture Mechanics*. Englewood Cliffs, New Jersey: Prentice Hall.

Wallace, Kelly. "A 'Confidence Code' for Girls: 5 Ways to Build up Our Daughters." *CNN*, May 21st, 2018, https://www.cnn.com/2018/05/21/health/girls-confidence-code-parenting/index.html.

Warrick, D.D. "What Leaders can Learn about Teamwork and Developing High Performance Teams from Organization Development Practitioners," *Performance Improvement* 55, no. 3 (2016): 13-21.

Wildman, Edwin. *Famous Leaders of Industry: The Life Stories of Boys who have Succeeded.* Boston: Page Company, 1921.

Witherington, Ben III. *Work – A Kingdom Perspective.* Grand Rapids: Wm. B. Eerdmans Publishing Co., 2011.

Zhao, Di and Wenjun Cai. "When does Emotional Intelligence (EI) Benefit Team-Member Exchange? the Cross-Level Moderating Role of EI-Based Leader-Member Exchange Differentiation," *Career Development International* 26, no. 3 (2021): 391-414.

ABOUT THE AUTHOR

D r. Maddox is an author, speaker, ICF credentialed coach, and philanthropist who began her professional career at the Federal Bureau of Investigation (FBI) Headquarters in 1985. She worked for the General Accountability Office (GAO) in Washington, DC and Dallas, Texas before completing the last 24 years of her 31-year federal career in Atlanta. She managed new building construction, alterations, and renovations of 25+ million square feet of commercial office space in eight southeastern states for the General Services Administration (GSA) and the Internal Revenue Service (IRS).

Dr. Maddox regularly worked with the Federal Emergency Management Agency (FEMA) on hurricane deployment as a Contracting Officer with unlimited real property contract authority to sign emergency commercial leases during Hurricane Katrina. Also, Dr. Maddox engaged in a nine-month undercover operation after receiving a potential bribe of a federal contract. The bribery case was managed by Federal law enforcement agencies, resulting in the suspect's arrest during an undercover operation and takedown at the Hartsfield-Jackson

Atlanta International Airport. Dr. Maddox continued coaching managers and executives in the IRS Internal Executive Coaching Program until retirement.

Post-retirement, Dr. Maddox launched her executive, leadership, and business coaching practice and returned to Mississippi to care for family members. While in Mississippi, she was ordained as a minister by Pastor Jonathan W. Hopkins and taught culinary enthusiasts at the Viking Cooking School.

Dr. Maddox currently coaches c-suite executives, managers, entrepreneurs, and high-potentials in Fortune 50, 100, and 500 companies in the United States and 45 countries. She is available for speaking engagements, private coaching, and keynotes.

INDEX

information, 6, 11, 16, 17, 25, 31, 37, 43, 44, 59, 63, 64, 66, 69
innovation, 16, 35
integrity, 27, 52
intelligence quotient, 41
international, 2, 9, 19, 31, 32, 58, 77, 78, 92
Internet, 43, 57
inventions, 4
invest, 4, 30, 37, 66, 75, 76
investment, 20, 21, 37, 42, 62, 63

K

kingdom, 3, 50, 69, 70, 79, 81
knowledge, 2, 4, 7, 14, 16, 46, 50, 51, 58, 59, 73, 75, 76, 77

L

labor, 54, 63, 67, 71, 72, 73
land, 5, 12, 69
leaders, v, 1, 5, 8, 8, 10, 14, 16, 17, 19, 20, 21, 22, 23, 24, 26, 27, 29, 32, 33, 34, 36, 37, 38, 39, 40, 41, 45, 46, 47, 50, 52, 54, 56, 58, 63, 64, 65, 66, 67, 68, 73, 74, 75, 77, 79, 80, 81
leadership, ix, 2, 3, 4, 7, 8, 10, 11, 13, 16, 20, 21, 23, 24, 26, 27, 29, 34, 36, 41, 46, 54, 57, 75, 78, 92
kingdom leadership, 3
lessons, 7, 9, 19

M

media, 42, 43, 44
mental, 11, 17, 23, 41, 43, 44, 61, 63, 73, 76
mentor, 20, 35
mentors, 2, 32, 34, 65

mentorship, 77
millionaire, 16
ministry, 27, 74
mischievousness, 10
money, 6, 30, 37, 65, 74, 76, 77
morals, 21, 22, 23

N

negotiation, ix, 9, 10, 13, 26, 33, 60, 61, 62, 63, 64, 65
nerve cells, 11, 16
network, 16
neural, 11, 16
neurologists, 63

O

opportunity, 4, 11, 18, 34, 42, 46, 47, 50, 63, 75, 83, 86, 90, 92
organization, 38, 77
organizations, 14, 21, 25, 26, 64, 77

P

pandemic, 2, 33, 34, 35, 42, 44, 45
parent, 6, 10, 27, 51, 65
partnerships, 2, 3
patent, 14, 15
performance, 1, 19, 24, 25, 26, 27, 37, 38, 43
power, 11, 22, 23, 39, 47, 55
problem-solving, 8, 10,
prosperity, 5, 69, 71, 74, 76, 77
prosperous, 69
prototypes, 17
psychologists, 17
purpose, 3, 20, 23, 24, 32, 33, 38, 40, 45, 46, 50, 52, 63, 66, 68, 70, 71, 73, 74

www.ingramcontent.com/pod-product-compliance
Lightning Source LLC
Chambersburg PA
CBHW062007040426
42447CB00010B/1948